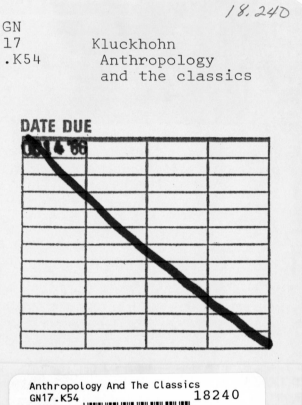

ANTHROPOLOGY *and the* CLASSICS

THE COLVER LECTURES
IN BROWN UNIVERSITY
1960

The Charles K. Colver Lectureship was established in 1915 by Mr. and Mrs. Jesse L. Rosenberger in honor of Mrs. Rosenberger's father Charles Kendrick Colver, of the class of 1842.

ANTHROPOLOGY
and the
CLASSICS

By

CLYDE KLUCKHOHN

PROVIDENCE, RHODE ISLAND

Brown University Press
1961

Library of Congress Catalog Card Number: 61-11106

FOREWORD

CLYDE K. M. KLUCKHOHN, Professor of Anthropology and Curator of Southwestern American Ethnology in the Peabody Museum, Harvard University, died in Sante Fe, New Mexico, on July 29, 1960, at the age of fifty-five.

In April of that year, Professor Kluckhohn delivered the Charles K. Colver Lectures at Brown University. As is the custom, the lectures were three in number, spread over several days. During his sojourn on our campus, the charm and brilliance of his personality, and the vast learning which he carried so lightly, endeared him to all. It was a time, too, when former students, now on the Brown faculty, delighted to recall not only their professional debt to him but also the countless little things which he had characteristically troubled to do for them over the years.

Professor Kluckhohn's lectures made a deep impression on the audience, for it was clear that here was a man who had a profound understanding of the ancient Greeks and yet might just as easily have lectured on the anthropological background of another civilization, as indeed his entire life bore witness.

C. A. ROBINSON, JR.

Contents

ANTHROPOLOGY *and the* CLASSICS

I   Historical Retrospect

AN ANALYSIS of the total relationship between anthropology and the study of classic civilizations is too vast an undertaking —as I realized to my cost after I had committed myself to it. Some arbitrary restrictions must at once be made. I shall deal exclusively with Greek materials; and shall allude only incidentally to relevant work in three of the major anthropological specialties: physical anthropology, archaeology, and linguistics. Even so, I shall necessarily be immensely selective rather than comprehensive. I only hope that the audience will remember that I am painfully aware how much must be left out of consideration.

My subject centers, then, upon the mutual interplay between studies of Greek antiquity and studies in ethnology and social anthropology. In what ways has classical scholarship stimulated anthropological investigation? What concepts and premises have the classicists, in their turn, borrowed from anthropology? How can contemporary anthropology best use the storehouse of Greek data? These will be the central questions for exploration here.

Engaging though the task would be, one cannot easily undertake to examine the consequences for anthropology of the fact that a number of the most influential of American anthropologists have been well read in Greek and Latin literature. My teacher and former colleague, E. A. Hooton, took his Ph.D. in the classics, and a few of his early publications are in classical art and archaeology. Franz Boas went through the classical gymnasium before going on to a doctorate in physics, and we know that his interest in manners and customs was stimulated by his study of Herodotus, Thucydides, Caesar, and others. A. L. Kroeber has much to say of Greek literature, philosophy, and the arts in his *Configurations of Culture Growth* (1944) and in his paper on "The Historical Oikumene" (1946), and elsewhere one encounters the evidences of his classical background. Nevertheless, Greek culture was not a prime preoccupation of any of these men, and I must leave them aside, together with those classicists who occasionally and incidentally refer to anthropological fact or anthropological theory. Similarly, I must neglect those Hellenists who have provided us with excellent ethnographies of one or more periods of classic culture: the work of such men as Seymour on the Homeric age; Blegen, Francis Cornford, Arthur Evans, Warde Fowler, Jarde, F. B. Jevons, Gardner, Gulick, D. M. Robinson, and others. I seek for those instances where the meeting of the two streams of research and thought was momentous, where the subsequent history and present position of the two disciplines was different because the streams met.

I shall begin with an historical retrospect. It is well known that many of the pioneer anthropologists were either classicists or had a background in classical studies. It is equally true that many of the leading students of ancient Greece in the late nineteenth and early twentieth centuries were profoundly influenced by ideas emanating from the developing science of anthropology.

In the tone of historical perspective, it might be well to point out at this juncture that among many of the world's leading anthropologists, Herodotus has been acepted as having been the first anthropologist. He was the first to try to record carefully the customs and habits of peoples other than his own, and his interest and comment is not incompatible with what might be done by many contemporary anthropologists.

In Germany the so-called "philological ethnologists," such as Usener and Rohde, engaged in work inspired by E. B. Tylor's theory of animism. Hermann Usener (1834-1905) published an anthropological and psychological classification of deities and their origin and evolution (1904). Gods of one type were held to designate a single awesome phenomenon such as lightning. The others signified a class of phenomena such as thunder. Usener maintained that this latter type of deity evolved into a personal god when the divine name was no longer intelligible because of changes in the language. Erwin Rohde (1845-1898) dealt with the cult of the souls and the belief in immortality among the Greeks. He emphasized the importance of primitive religion and folklore in the understanding of Greek religion. He traced the origin of the belief in immortality to the ecstatic cults. He postulated shamanistic elements in Greek culture—a theme to which the Regius Professor of Greek in Oxford (E. R. Dodds) has quite recently returned and developed.

Under the stimulus of the "philological ethnologists," Jane Harrison (1850-1928) attributed much in popular Greek religion to the worship of ghosts and underworld spirits. Her later work, *Themis: a Study of the Social Origins of Greek Religion* (1912), derives much from Durkheim and his school. She tries to deduce certain Greek rites from initiation ceremonies and to trace gods to "projections" of the society. In her final book, "projection" is treated both in an anthropological and psychoanalytic fashion.

Sir William Ridgeway (1853-1926) held firmly to one anthropological viewpoint that was rare among the classicists of his day. They ordinarily insisted on viewing Greek culture as a magnificent but lonely island, possibly touched a bit by the high civilizations of Crete, Egypt, and the Near East. Ridgeway was comparative and did not despise evidence from the barbarians. To good effect he ridiculed the followers of Muller who attempted to explain everything in mythology and much in ritual from the habit of talking metaphorically about the weather. He argued that the almost universal human belief in the immortality of the soul is primary. Totemism depends on this premise. Men pray first to their ancestors, not to abstract spirits. Greek tragedy arose out of dramatic dances in honor of the dead.

These four figures, two German and two British, may serve as examples of classical scholars in an earlier period who dealt with anthropological matters and used anthropological ideas.

E. B. Tylor, the acknowledged leader of British anthropology for fifty years and the first professor of anthropology in a British university, used classical data in his own writings only as one aspect of a comparative approach. His interest is, however, attested in a number of ways. In 1888 he gave a course of lectures on "Anthropological Elucidation of Passages in Greek and Latin Authors." This series was followed by courses on: Anthropology as Related to Ancient and Modern History, The Anthropology of Higher Nations, Anthropology in Classical Literature, Anthropology in Ancient History, and similar titles. The *Festschrift* presented to Tylor in 1907 contains four essays based on Greek and Latin materials. Two of the students who followed some of Tylor's lectures that I have just listed turned from classics to anthropology: J. L. Myres and R. R. Marett. However, of those who were influenced by Tylor and his work to turn from classical studies to make a metier of anthropology the two most famous made the change still earlier: Andrew Lang (1844-1912) and James George Frazer (1854-1941).

Lang sought, first of all, a key to classical origins. His basic premise was an evolutionary one: all civilization represents evolved savagery. He tilted with Max Muller and others who considered myth a "disease of language." Like an anthropologist, he saw Greek Culture as a specific manifestation of a greater phenomenon, climactic but still only a phase in the growth of culture generally. Many of his specific findings also have the flavor of the anthropology of his time. Originally a follower of Tylor, Lang in his *The Making of Religion* (1898) broke with the animistic theory of the evolution of religion. He saw "high gods" among exceedingly primitive peoples. Theism of an ethical character did not originate in any form of animistic belief. These heterodoxies made him unpopular with other British anthropologists and his later studies of exogamy and totemism received little attention. To the end of his life Lang was both Hellenist and anthropologist.

Frazer, however, came to devote himself wholly to anthropology, though it was definitely a humanistic anthropology. His first major work was on Pausanias. After that he explored the pan-human universe of rite and belief. His books on totemism and exogamy, on the folklore of the Old Testament, and the twelve volumes of the famous *Golden Bough* (1890) constitute an organized storehouse of information through space and time on magic, taboo, fertility cults, dying gods, conceptions of immortality, sacrifices, scapegoats, and the like. As Freud mapped with bold sweep the terrain of the unconscious and irrational, so Frazer gave us fresh and imaginative charts of the non-rational area of human behavior—the customary.

Frazer's work had enormous influence, reaching far beyond the small circles having a specialized interest in comparative religion and anthropology. The ornate splendor and felicity of his writing attracted laymen and literary people as well as scholars. His interpretations of recurrent regularities in human thinking drew the attention of philosophers, psychologists, psychiatrists, sociologists, and men of affairs. There is little doubt that Frazer has been more widely read than any other anthropologist, and his impact upon other outstanding men was tremendous; Freud, T. S. Eliot, and James Joyce are some notable examples.

But in the professional camp the inevitable reaction set in. Frazer became looked down upon as a compiler who did not always scrutinize his sources very carefully. He adhered to a falsely rationalistic psychology. He did not keep up with advances in anthropological theory. These and other more detailed criticisms were well founded. Yet it would be a mistake to dismiss the *Golden Bough* today as a wealthy vein of antiquarian ore to be mined for delightful curiosities. While aspects of his theory are outmoded, there are others where contemporary anthropology is only just coming abreast of him. This is notably the case with respect to Frazer's insistence that human universals are as much of a fact as are cultural variations. During most of this century anthropologists have stressed the gamut of variability, pointed out the exceptions to every generalization proposed, and made few empirical inquiries as to possible highest common factors or least common denominators. Only lately has there been much recognition that the facts of anthropology attest that the phrase "a common humanity" has veridical meaning and importance. To be sure, most of the resemblances are very broad, very general, all too easily obscured by the external trappings of custom. Nevertheless, cultures are many; man is one. Frazer saw this with complete clarity:

On the one hand, the essential similarity of man's chief wants everywhere and at all times, and on the other hand, the wide difference between the means he has adopted to satisfy them in different ages (Frazer, 1959, p. 648).

I shall return to Frazer and his followers among the Hellenists and among the anthropologists, but first a review of another major theme of nineteenth century studies: social organization. Frazer and his predecessors were concerned mainly with the broad subjects of religion and folklore. The interest in social structure was largely introduced by five jurists and historians who were not professional classicists but who used classical data extensively in anthropological directions.

J. J. Bachofen (1815-1887) in his book on mother-right (1861) starts from Herodotus' account of the Lycians as matrilineal and reconstructs a whole social system which, he maintains, antedated the patriarchal society of classical antiquity. Women ruled the household and the state by virtue of the fact that they were the earthly representatives of female fertility deities. A form of social organization, a form of religion, and a type of subsistence (agriculture) are taken as closely associated. As an evolutionist, Bachofen postulated a sequence of universal stages: primeval promiscuity was followed by a revolt of the women which led to mother-right; this was succeeded by the "higher" stage of matriarchy. While Bachofen draws parallels from non-literate societies, he rests his case primarily on classical data. The whole book teems with references to classical mythology and is studded with Greek and Latin quotations.

The American, Lewis H. Morgan (1818-1881), was a

lawyer turned anthropologist who has a place of great importance in the history of studies of social structure and indeed of anthropology in general. He devotes many pages in his *Ancient Society* (1877) to comparisons of Greek and Roman social organization with that of the Iroquois Indians. In his *Systems of Consanguinity and Affinity* (1870) he treats the kinship systems of Greece and Rome.

Sir Henry Maine (1822-1888) I shall mention, although his materials were almost exclusively Roman. However, *Ancient Law* (1861) contains some germs of modern anthropological method and, even before Morgan, Maine drew the distinction between kinship, or tribal, organization and territorial, or political, organization. For Maine, in contrast to Bachofen, Morgan, and others, the patriarchal family was the basic unit of primitive social organization.

John McLennan (1827-1881) treated Spartan marriage ceremonies as symbolic behavior that was a survival of previous actual relationships, in this case marriage by capture. He dealt with many forms of social organization such as the levirate and polyandry. His terms, endogamy and exogamy, became permanently incorporated in the lexicon of social anthropology.

Fustel de Coulanges (1830-1889) in *La Cité Antique* (1864) stressed the differences between classical and later forms of jurisprudence. His treatment of names, private property, and other features of Greek culture had an impact upon Morgan, particularly on the latter's notions of the clan. Fustel de Coulanges likewise influenced anthropological theory as regards "functionalism." He asserted that all institutions must be considered in a wide context: law, for instance, cannot be understood apart from religion.

The interest in law and social organization and the interest in religion and folklore converged in one common intellectual matrix, that of evolution. Bachofen, Fustel de Coulanges, Harrison, and others sometimes took the position which recent anthropology has termed "functionalism." That is, they showed interest in how societies worked, in the mutual interrelations of culture patterns. But the persistent concern was with origins, survivals, stages.

Labels are libels, yet we need them. In studies of anthropology and the classics in this century one may properly distinguish two streams. The first exhibits a rough continuity from Usener, Rohde, Bachofen; from Ridgeway, Harrison, Lang, Frazer, and the rest down to the present day. E. E. Sikes' pleasant and informative little book, *The Anthropology of the Greeks* (1914), belongs in this stream. So does A. R. Burn's *The World of Hesiod* (1936) though Burn draws a bit from nonevolutionary anthropologists and even from two psychoanalysts (Freud and Ernest Jones). There are, of course, modifications, enlargements, reservations and qualifications. But there has also been an unbroken succession. The second stream, arising from the "new look" in anthropology, represents a fairly sharp discontinuity. The division is not, one must note, strictly chronological. Ridgeway and Harrison lived well into this century. Frazer did not die until 1941 and Gilbert Murray still later. But the mold of thought of all these and others was dominantly and indelibly of nineteenth century cast.

There continued to be many classical anthropological classicists, such as Sir John Myres, author of *Who Were the Greeks?* (1930), and anthropological classicists, such as R. M. Dawkins, and notably in Britain. I shall choose for brief comment those figures who are from the English-speaking world. This leaves out important continental scholars such

11

as Glotz who published extensively on Greek law, the Greek family, mythology, trial by ordeal, and other topics of anthropological concern. But Glotz' work is the continuation of that of Fustel de Coulanges, and Glotz' approach is historical and sociological rather than anthropological. Similar remarks would hold for certain publications in German. In the twentieth century I believe that the mainstream of the interchange which I wish to follow out lies indeed in the English-speaking world.

Perhaps I may begin with two of my teachers, Gilbert Murray and R. R. Marett. Both may be regarded as disciples of Sir James Frazer. Murray will dispute a datum or a specific interpretation with Frazer, but he adheres basically to Frazer's conceptual framework—as, for instance, in *Five Stages of Greek Religion* (1925). Marett, a classicist turned anthropologist, diverged further. He admired both Frazer and Tylor (whose successor he was at Oxford), but he rejected their intellectualism. He emphasized the non-rational determinants of group behavior and belief. With the French school he saw that religion serves the functions of maintaining solidarity and restoring confidence in crisis but, more than the French, he recognized the complexity of religious phenomena. His point of view was still to some degree evolutionary but he insisted that we must ask: *how and why* do survivals occur? Marett's contemporary, H. J. Rose, likewise pointed to the complexity of the phenomena and repudiated the attempt to explain everything in history by reference to the "primitive." It was too hasty a deduction that *all* magic and religion began with the invocation of spirits. Rose, by academic title a professor of Greek but by the bulk of his work an anthropologist or folklorist, was quite explicit that one could not get a valid chronological order of "stages" by "the simple process of putting first one which seemed simplest to them, and so in succession . . ." (1934, p. 5). He also said:

In the form it sometimes assumed a generation or two ago, Evolutionism is as dead as anything deserves to be which is the baseborn offspring of a promiscuous horde of paralogisms (1934, p. 4).

On the other hand, Rose held to the comparative method and the Frazerian postulate that men are much the same, the world over.

Marett and Rose seem to have been the last anthropologists who worked largely along Frazerian lines. But among the classicists, one can point to works published in the last fifteen years which are still essentially Frazerian in viewpoint. As illustrations I mention an example from each side of the Atlantic. In his book (1946) on the Homeric epics, Carpenter employs a comparative method similar to that of Frazer and which indeed has some affinities to Max Muller. R. B. Onians in his massive *Origins of European Thought* (1951; 2nd ed., 1954) cites new archaeological work and is far more careful with his sources than Frazer. Nevertheless his most recent authority in social anthropology is Frazer, and the tone of his text is reminiscent of Frazer.

There is also continuity from the current of law and social organization. George Thomson in *Aeschylus and Athens* (1941) and *Studies in Ancient Greek Society* (1949) is aware of many of the "moderns": Kroeber, Lowie, Firth, Malinowski, Radcliffe-Brown. But he rejects them in favor of doctrinaire Marxist anthropology based upon Morgan and Engels. He has chapters on totemism, matriarchy, and "communism." He sees the origins of Greek drama in social and economic pressures. His discussions of totemism and matrilineal descent recall equally Morgan and Frazer. Some of the same ideas, though put in more qualified and more sophisticated form, appear in Alan Little's *Myth and Society in Attic Drama* (1942).

I would, however, take Little's book as approximately at the watershed between the Hellenists' use of the "old" and the "new" anthropology. On the one hand, he takes Morgan as trustworthy anthropology and is still interested in totemism, the evolution of matrilineal to patrilineal descent in Greece, and in origins generally. On the other hand, Little relies heavily upon Malinowski for his interpretations of Greek myths and invokes "modern" as well as nineteenth century explanations of social function.

What are the principal differences between the "old" and the "new" anthropology? For purposes relevant here I think we may list the following:

1. Extreme skepticism as regards *simpliste* evolutionary schemes and attendant diminished interest in origins.
2. The premises that cultures have organization as well as content, and that the distinctiveness of each culture rests in its patterned selectivity.
3. Focus upon each culture as a network of patterns which both increase and restrict human potentialities.
4. Stress upon the non-rational aspects of cultures; every culture constitutes a bar to the free exercise of rationality.
5. Enlargement of anthropological theory by the incorporation of a good deal of psychology, particularly Freudian psychology.

Turning now to the application of this "new" anthropology, to the data of Grecian antiquity, there is little choice among the anthropologists. Unhappily only a few have made forays into the classical field. The work of substance in the past generation has been done by archaeologists like my colleague, Hugh Hencken (*Indo-European Languages and Archaeology,* 1955) and physical anthropologists like J. L. Angel.

14

Hencken and Angel know Greek. Few of their contemporaries in social anthropology and ethnology do. Nevertheless there have been some contributions which, though of slight magnitude, are of interest.

Raymond Firth (1958, pp. 7-10) points to the lack of systematic study of the Greek "kin-bound" society. He suggests that the *Oresteia* contains a symbolic, a religious affirmation of the social principle of patrilineality. In further discussing the ritual and social sanctions for conduct, he calls attention to the elaborate network of obligations in Homeric society and the importance of the patterned exchange of gifts. Firth is impressed by the resemblance of Homeric culture to that of Polynesia and other non-literate cultures. He sees the real value of the study of Greek culture not so much in understanding the origins of our own as in providing a set of contrasts to contemporary Western culture.

Meyer Fortes, in his charming little book, *Oedipus and Job in West African Religion* (1959) uses the stories of Oedipus and Orestes as background for a comparative study. But in contrast to Frazer's basis of superficial features, Fortes is analytic. What is significant in the tale of Orestes is that he murdered a *kinswoman,* that this kinswoman was his *mother,* that his expiation was to mutilate himself *by biting off a finger.* To Frazer, the point was the illustration of a particular kind of barbarous superstition: fear of ghosts acting as a curb on would-be murderers. To Fortes, the point is conceptual: from the story of Orestes and similar tales can we derive general principles, a model or paradigm of apparently irrational mutilations carried out in the context of an overt or suppressed conflict between successive generations?

Lévi-Strauss likewise in his analysis of the Oedipus myth (1955) tries to get at least common factors or highest common denominators which he takes to be implicit in the descriptive content. He is seeking constituent units, comparable to the phonemes or morphemes of language, which would be comparable cross-culturally. Each gross constituent unit consists in a relation, but the bundle of such relations (analogous to the bundle of distinctive features in phonology) defines the implicit conceptual content of the myth. Lévi-Strauss' "translation" of the Oedipus story is that it rests upon two pairs of polar oppositions: 1) over-rating of blood relations vs. under-rating of blood relations; 2) denial of the autochthonous nature of man vs. the persistence of the authochthonous nature of man. His argument is involved and perhaps strained. It would take too long even to summarize it here. Classicists and indeed anthropologists will probably not altogether accept it. But what is relevant to my discourse is that Lévi-Strauss, in fashion characteristic of the "new anthropology," strives to go beneath the surface of custom, beyond "common sense" entities in order to make possible a genuinely comparative science of culture.

On the Hellenist side, there is more choice. I shall limit myself to hasty notes upon two representative works, reserving longer commentary for one book that seems to me of outstanding importance in the realm of general ideas.

M. I. Finley's *The World of Odysseus* (1954) will strike the anthropologist who chances to read it as a first-rate piece of ethnography reconstructed from literary sources. It is precisely the kind of thing which I should like to see anthropologists who know Greek produce. A reading of his text shows how well abreast of contemporary anthropological thought he is. And the sources from which he has drawn this knowledge are indicated in his "bibliographical essay."

Norman Brown's *Hermes the Thief* (1947) is more severely

technical in apparatus. But it is likewise excellent ethnography. His chapters on tribal customs and on the various Greek periods with which he deals are at least as well documented as monographs based on field expeditions. Brown's treatment of myth is informed both by the studies of Frazer and by those of Malinowski and other later writers. His discussion of primitive trade draws upon the appropriate anthropological sources.

The Greeks and the Irrational (1951) by E. R. Dodds has impressed me as much as any book I have read in a decade. His anthropological interests and sophistication were evidenced earlier in his edition of the *Bacchae* of Euripides where he did not hesitate to draw parallels from the Kwakiutl Indians, the Polynesians, and other "primitives" to illuminate the relations of symbolism to social structure, the comparative cultural psychology of maenadism, and other topics.

Allow me to summarize portions of his argument in his last book. Homeric civilization was what anthropologists call a "shame culture." Forbidden and irrational impulses were externalized upon gods and demons. The subsequent Archaic Age shows a transformation into a "guilt culture" conditioned by the tensions arising from the growing claim of the individual in a compact family organization. Family solidarity explains the fact that the father's guilt, just as his debts, can be inherited by the son. Such a world needs divine assurance as provided by ecstatic prophecy, especially at Delphi, in order to overcome the "crush of human ignorance and human insecurity." But it also needs Dionysiac and similar rites which purge the individual of infectuous irrational impulses.

The cultural determination of subconscious phenomena is evidenced by Greek lore regarding dreams, especially the appearance of a god, priest, parent, or other person who like

17

Asclepius during the temple sleep reveals events (without symbolism) and extends help and advice. In these cases, the dream experience of the patients also reveals their unconscious attitudes toward their diseases. If by the end of the fifth century B.C. "orphic" opinions hold dreams to be signs of the "innate power of the soul itself" (Dodds, p. 118), this is a manifestation of a new religious pattern, the "puritanical." Its origin goes back to the closer contact with shamanistic cultures around the Black Sea in the seventh century. Shamanism with its individualistic religious experience of an occult self of divine origin "appealed to the growing individualism of an age for which the collective ecstacies of Dionysus were no longer wholly sufficient" (p. 142). Shamanism favored the belief in reincarnation but also promoted revulsion against the body and condemnation of pleasure. Purity, brought about by magical techniques, became "the cardinal means of salvation" (p. 154).

The classical age thus had Murray's "inherited conglomerate" of various official and unofficial religious concepts and beliefs. The Sophistic enlightenment with its roots in sixth century Ionia threatened to dissolve it, and the rationalism of the Sophists brought with it "a sense of liberation . . . from meaningless rules and irrational guilt feelings" (p. 189). Yet rationalism had its dangers. It enabled men "to justify their brutality to themselves"; moreover, "the divorce between the beliefs of the few and the beliefs of the many was made absolute" (p. 192). The popular reaction evidenced itself "in the successful prosecutions of intellectuals on religious grounds which took place at Athens in the last third of the fifth century" (p. 189). Plato attempted to stabilize the dangerous situation inherent in the decay of the "inherited conglomerate." He equated human reason, the "rational Socratic *psyche*," with the detachable occult self of shamanistic tradition, accepted "the poet, the prophet, and the 'corybantic' as being in some sense channels of divine or daemonic grace" (p. 218), and proposed reforms that were to culminate in a "new State Church . . . , a joint cult of Apollo and the sun-god Helios . . . Apollo standing for the traditionalism of the masses, and Helios for the new 'natural religion' of the philosophers" (p. 221). However, Plato failed, and the dissolution of the conglomerate proceeded.

One does not have to accept this argument completely to find it a brilliant union of humanistic and anthropological scholarship. I myself have my reservations. Dodds sometimes forgets that "shame culture" and "guilt culture" are "ideal types" (in Max Weber's sense). Nor can Apollonian ecstatic prophecy be distinguished as sharply from shamanistic experience as does Professor Dodds. And I find his derivation of Greek shamanism from the Scythians anthropologically improbable. But these and numerous other objections in no way alter the fact that this is a profoundly innovating and a great book. It makes me ashamed to recall that my shift from the classics to anthropology was on the ostensible ground that all of the interesting work on Greece had already been done!

The fact that such a book could be published by the Regius Professor of Greek in Oxford suggests to me that the case for anthropological ideas and for comparative studies of non-literate and non-Greek peoples as helping us to understand Greek civilization has been at least partly won. I have looked up a good many reviews by classicists of *The Greeks and the Irrational*. Some were admittedly pained in tone, and others were grudging. But none that were read said, in effect, "This is monstrous. There is nothing at all to it."

In contrast, the writings of Frazer and Murray, their contemporaries and predecessors, did not at all please the more conservative Hellenists. One reads many harsh epithets. I shall quote as representative an outraged protest from Professor Paul Shorey:

> Professor Murray has done much harm by helping to substitute in the minds of an entire generation for Arnold's and Jebb's conception of the serene rationality of the classics the corybantic Hellenism of Miss Harrison and Isadora Duncan and Susan Glaspell and Mr. Stark Young's "Good Friday and Classical Professors," the higher vaudeville Hellenism of Mr. Vachel Lindsay, the anthropological Hellenism of the disciples of Sir James Frazer, the irrational, semi-sentimental, Polynesian, free-verse and sex-freedom Hellenism of all the gushful geysers of "rapturous rubbish" about the Greek spirit.

To this line of attack, Dodds, of course, retorts vigorously that the Greeks were not so serenely rational after all.

Not dissimilar is the trend of a number of books published in the 1950's on the dramatists. Victorian and Edwardian scholarship, alike in Britain and in Germany, strongly tended to expunge or to explain primitivism away. But now the so-called "theology" is quite generally seen as a good deal more primitive and Hesiodic or even Homeric than the chorus of earlier authorities would allow. Mr. S. M. Adams still believes firmly that Aeschylus was a monotheist and strives to discover a semi-Christian eschatology in the *Oedipus at Colonus*. But Cedric Whitman in his book on Sophocles which appeared a few years earlier takes quite a contrary position. Richmond Lattimore (who observes that the *Oedipus Tyrannus* is another foundling story) also makes it plain that Sophocles is far less saturated with Victorian sweetness and light than we had supposed. Mr. Hugh Lloyd-Jones has stripped Aeschylus' Zeus of the quasi-Christian mask clamped on him by the Oxford Movement and put him firmly back in his crude ritual setting.

Recent relations between classical archaeology and anthropology are somewhat curious. The classical archaeologists have drawn on physical anthropologists such as J. Lawrence Angel. There are a few anthropological archaeologists such as Hugh Hencken who have maintained good communication with the classical archaeologists. But classical archaeology has never become one of the sub-disciplines of the general science of anthropology as has prehistoric archaeology. It has remained largely autonomous, apart, affiliated principally with the main body of Hellenic studies—i.e. a grouping along substantive rather than disciplinary lines. This, I think, is because classical archaeology has remained a pure humanistic discipline, while anthropology is only partially humanistic.

And it is in the stronghold of the traditional humanism, classical philology, that modern anthropological thinking has penetrated least. For instance, the 1955 inaugural lecture of the new professor of classical philology at Oxford, L. R. Palmer, is devoted to the social organization and polity of the Achaeans but makes no reference to recent anthropological work in social structure. He does quote casually the anthropological archaeologist, V. Gordon Childe.

Nevertheless, on the whole, contemporary classical scholarship is receptive to the following anthropological notions: 1) Greece and even Greek literature cannot profitably be studied in a cultural vacuum. 2) There is much more of the "primitive" in classical Greece than was heretofore acknowledged by most Hellenists. 3) Some ideas from anthropology and psychology can illuminate Greek data.

From this rather arid listing of names and contributions, let us turn, finally, to a matter of broad interpretative interest.

Starting with a mutual *rapprochement,* the flow of ideas and materials between the two fields of classics and anthropology has become over the years increasingly one-sided. Hellenists turn frequently to anthropology, possibly more in the past fifteen years than since the first two decades of this century. The reverse is not true. There are, I think, two principal reasons. The first is the simple—and regrettable—fact of the language barrier. The second is that "armchair anthropology" is out of fashion. Professional prestige goes to those who work among living peoples, not to those scholars who cull their facts from musty books. However, despite the dearth of certain kinds of information which anthropologists urgently need, the available documentation on Greek antiquity is so rich that we are by-passing tremendously inviting opportunities to try our skills which are, hopefully, maturing.

But it is the third reason which may properly engage our reflection. Classicists are moving in the anthropological direction, I believe, because the wider intellectual climate of our times favors generalizations and principles as opposed to particulars, theory in contrast to description; science, if you like, as opposed to the humanities.

In his introduction to *Anthropology and the Classics* (1908), R. R. Marett intimated that in practice the humanities and anthropology divided the domain of human culture between them. Roughly, the humanities dealt with the civilized peoples and anthropology with the primitive. And Marett urged that the joint effort of the two fields be devoted to "the phenomena of transition," such as early Greek culture.

Today most of us would put the substance rather differently. In the first place, anthropologists would resist the identification of their subject with a kind of "higher barbarology." Indeed at least as far back as Tylor many have insisted that, in principle, anthropology was concerned with all mankind throughout space and time, and that it was only the urgency of disappearing or rapidly changing cultures that forced them to concentrate upon the non-literate peoples. In the second place, there are the social sciences which were virtually absent in the Oxford of 1908. Sociology was not represented at all, economics hardly so. Political science was assimilated to philosophy; history was an humanity.

However, I wish to focus upon the relation between anthropology and the humanities of which classical studies are the oldest and the outstanding example. Anthropology, properly speaking, is not a social science, though it is often called one today. It does contain social science elements, now alike as regards viewpoint, method, and content. Historically, however, it derives from the natural sciences, on the one hand, and the humanities, on the other. The first who may be called anthropologists as such were trained as physicians, natural historians, comparative anatomists, geologists—or as classicists, historians, and philosophers. The background of contemporary cultural anthropology is to be found in the Greeks and in Renaissance humanists such as Montaigne (cf. especially the essay on "the Cannibals"), Boemus, Pico della Mirandola, Pufendorf. Quite directly cultural anthropology stems from the Age of Enlightenment: from Montesquieu, de Brosses, Voltaire, Condorcet, Herder. The "social sciences" are later. Adam Smith's *The Wealth of Nations* (1776) may be taken as a starting point. Comte, the first sociologist, flourished some sixty years later. "Political Science" was still slower to disengage itself from history, law, and philosophy; moreover, the stream followed different channels. Social science from its beginnings was frankly ameliorative and utilitarian in intent. It did not depart from disinterested intellectual curiosity about man but rather from an urge to improve the human condition. This is true of Comte as well as of Marx. Social scientists from the beginning have cared more about the "ought" than the "is." The proto-anthropologists and the first anthropologists, on the other hand, were merely curious. They, like the humanists and the natural scientists, had a detached interest in the phenomena as such. Humanists and anthropologists approached values as *ta onta*—the things that are. Social scientists directed themselves toward social and cultural reality with the hope of changing it.

Actually as well as historically anthropology is a hybrid monster, as is attested by the fact that, alone among the disciplines, anthropology is represented in the national councils of the humanities, the natural sciences, and the social sciences. At least until very recently, anthropology was closer in its primitive postulates and primitive categories to both the natural sciences and the humanities than to the social sciences. This circumstance, it seems, is essential to a comprehension of past and present relations between the classics and anthropology.

A. L. Kroeber and Claude Lévi-Strauss (Tax *et al.*, 1953) agree that the natural sciences and the humanities share one important quality: they work in depth. Their search is intensive. They do not limit themselves to artificially created, isolated enclaves of study but rather try to take everything relevant into consideration. By comparison, the social sciences have not inquired seriously into fundamentals. Economics and political science deal with human behavior and the products of human behavior. Yet, with few, though increasing, exceptions, they have operated as if human biology, human psychology, human cultures were not germane to the problems or could be taken as approximate constants.

Kroeber further suggests that "anthropology largely represents an unconscious effort of total natural science to extend itself over the area traditionally held by the humanities." This may seem like an imperialistic claim of anthropology, and the statement should doubtless be qualified in various respects, but it strikes me that Kroeber is basically right. He proposes the development of anthropological linguistics out of philology as an early paradigm of what may be considerably extended in the future. Philology was an humanity—"interested in certain endless particulars of letters considered valuable in themselves and recognizing a hierarchy of languages, of forms, and of better and worse values." For all practical purposes, philology restricted itself to the tongues and literatures of the great civilizations. Anthropological linguistics, on the other hand, embraces all languages, seeking formulations of universal principles that have scientific elegance.

In an epoch when, for better or for worse, science is dominant on the intellectual horizon, it is not surprising that students of the oldest humanity find something congenial in that science which has—along with its scientific aspect—deep humanistic roots. In our days many Hellenists are men in search of a theory. They find some theoretical framework and some ideas suitable to their purposes in anthropology, especially that sector of anthropological thought which has incorporated some depth psychology.

II The Study of Man and a Man-Centered Culture

THE FIRST LECTURE outlined some of the long-continuing and mutually fruitful relations between the classics and anthropology. It was suggested that this happy circumstance could be attributed in some measure to an enduring humanistic component in anthropology. It is certainly the case that Hellenic studies have hardly had such ties with sociology or economics or psychology. Further, it was implied that the thought-ways of contemporary anthropology can be comprehended only in terms of the somewhat unusual conceptual genealogy of anthropology. In the writings of such Renaissance humanists as Pico della Mirandola, Boemus, and Montaigne one may discern more than a little foreshadowing of later anthropology. And who were these Humanists? They were the men who re-discovered for the modern West the first man-centered culture we know in history, that of the Greeks.

Did the Greeks have a genuine anthropology? When I first read Sir John Myres' (1907) statement that the Greeks were the first anthropologists I was frankly skeptical. I knew that Hecataeus had been termed the father of ethnology as well as the father of geography, that Herodotus had been called the father of anthropology as well as of history. But others had insisted that Lucretius or Pliny the Elder should be regarded as the first ancestor of the anthropologists. I suspected that Myres was trying to link his two loves in a connection which, if not false, was strained.

But now, after considerable study over the intervening years, I am fully persuaded that the lineage of contemporary anthropological thought traces straight back to Greek thought. Greek students of man and culture did not call themselves anthropologists. The *anthropologos* was, I am sorry to say, nothing more than a gossip or busybody. Probably some of those we study today give us—privately—the same description. Nevertheless, the Greeks did frame and try to answer many of the questions which we regard as important. Herodotus deserves the title of father of anthropology as well as of history because at the very beginning he says he will deal not only with what happened but also why it happened. It is as if, with the later historian, Eduard Meyer, he felt that the general interpretation of history is the task not of philosophy but of anthropology.

Every science has a side that is mainly descriptive and classificatory and a side where theoretical inquiry is dominant. It would be absurd to maintain that the Greeks were the first or the only people to manifest an interest in the physical type or the manners and customs of other groups. To remind you of two banal examples: there is the famous depiction in the Egyptian Middle Kingdom of the races of mankind, and there were the Chinese ethnographers who wrote about the Hiung-nu and other "barbarian" tribes. However, an attempt will be made to demonstrate that Greek descriptive anthropology was carried further and carried out more systematically than that of any other ancient people whose records have survived. Also, to the Greeks goes the credit of developing the beginnings of genuine anthropological theory. Hence their ethnography—at least after the sixth or perhaps one should say the fifth century B.C.—has a conceptual and not merely an antiquarian or historical viewpoint.

Let me give a running account of Greek anthropology, starting with their knowledge of peoples and places, their comments upon foreign ways, proceeding to Greek speculations upon matters of perennial human interest, and ending with some anticipations of contemporary theory.

Homer's world was largely that of the eastern Mediterranean basin. He did know of the "blameless Ethiopians" whom the Olympian gods visited for a twelve-day feast, the Abii (perhaps the Scythians), "the justest of men," who live in the north, and the mysterious Phaeacians. Homer showed little interest in the diversity of customs. He does remark that the Cyclopes lived without *themistes*—the established usages of mankind. In the eighth century, the ends of the earth for Hesiod are the Ethiopians, the mare-milking Scyths, and the Etruscans.

In the eighth and seventh centuries B.C. Greek travel and geographical knowledge were greatly enlarged. Greek settlements had been established from the furthest shores of the Euxine to the mouth of the Rhone and the eastern seaboard of Spain, in Egypt and in Cyrene. This period of voyaging and colonization undoubtedly gave an impetus to Greek anthropology—just as the emerging anthropology in the Age of the Enlightenment had as its background the excitement of the diverse cultural worlds in the Americas, the South Seas, Asia, and Africa, which were brought to European attention by the discoveries and travels of the sixteenth and seventeenth centuries. With the growth of the Persian empire, Greek merchants went as far as Susa. Before long, of course, the Greek geographical world extended from Cadiz to the Ganges. In the sixth century Anaximander made the first map we know of. A bit later Hecataeus wrote his *Description of the Earth*. Aeschylus—probably drawing on Hecataeus—refers to the Indians (camel-riding nomads), the Persians, the Egyptians, the Ethiopians, the Libyans, the Scythians. His ethnic criteria are cultural, not racial. In the *Persae* the two women of Atossa's dream are as alike as sisters in form and figure. But by their dress Atossa concludes that one is Persian, the other Greek. In the *Suppliants* costume and accessories are the criteria for saying that the women of the Danaid chorus are foreign. Language is invoked only when such customs are indecisive.

The *locus classicus* is, of course, the wide-eyed Herodotus. In addition to peoples mentioned by earlier writers, he discusses such groups as the Ligurians living inland from Marseilles and the Sigynnae who inhabited a part of what is now Romania. He is fascinated by cultural diversity: circumcision, avoidance of nakedness, performance of urination in private. As an anthropocentric Greek, he is a bit horrified to find that the Egyptians have animal-headed deities. But in typical Greek fashion he uses abstract concepts by postulation. He is a universalist. He equates Horus with Apollo, Osiris with Dionysus, Bupastis with Artemis. Yet he faithfully details the phenomenological variability. Like a good anthropologist, he is especially copious on sources of subsistence and on marriage customs.

The ethnic criteria of Herodotus are mainly cultural. In the passage where the Athenians reject the Macedonian proposals to desert the Pan-Hellenic cause, common descent, common language, common religion, and common customs are invoked. Elsewhere he quotes with approval Pindar's observation that "custom is king of all." He notes that the Greeks will under no circumstances eat the corpses of their fathers, nor the Indians cremate theirs. He reproaches Cambyses for violating "the long-established usages" of other peoples:

For if one were to offer men to choose out of all the customs in the world such as seemed to them the best, they would examine the whole number, and end by preferring their own; so convinced are they that their own usages far surpass those of all others. Unless, therefore, a man was mad, it is not likely that he would make light of such matters (III, 38; tr. Rawlinson).

Greek interest in describing the gamut of variability of human custom flowered after Herodotus also. Let me mention only some outstanding examples: the "Airs, Waters, and Places" portion of the writings attributed to Hippocrates; the *Cyropaedia* of Xenophon; Plato's comparative study of foreign customs in the *Laws;* the *nomina barbarika* of Aristotle. There are many passages highly reminiscent of nineteenth century anthropology. Plato's *Laws* is an outstanding case. Take, for instance, his discussion of drinking among various peoples (I, 637). Some writers, like Heracleitus and Aristotle, were disposed to look for the similarities beneath the trappings of custom—for universal human psychology or "raw human nature." Others stressed the differences. Theophrastus begins his *Characters* by saying: "Isn't it odd that we Greeks, who speak the same language and are brought up in about the same way, are nevertheless so variable psychologically?"

Let us move to speculations on matters which are inevitably of interest to the anthropologist. Greek views on human origins are inconsistent and singularly undogmatic. The Greeks were very open-minded. Homeric Zeus is "the father of Gods and men." Aristotle interpreted this as meaning simply a patriarchal king, but there are passages in Homer and other writers which could be adduced to support the notion of biological paternity. In the *Works and Days* Hesiod portrays some men as created by Zeus, others by earlier gods of the epoch of Chronos. The Orphics apparently believed that the human race sprang from mother-earth and father-heaven. There are notions of birth from stones and birth from trees. In the *Prometheus* of Aeschylus there is a hint of spontaneous generation. In brief, man was either autochthonous in some form or other or he was created by or descended from the gods. The Greeks did not seem greatly exercised by the issue.

They did, however, proceed to adumbrate the first known theories of evolution, both biological and cultural. Anaximander (born 611 B.C.) maintained that life must originate from lifeless matter somehow and in a gradual way. The action of the sun's heat on slime or sea water must have produced the simpler organisms. From the helplessness of newborn land animals, including human babies, he concluded that mammals cannot have been the earliest form of life. Fish give no further attention to their young—therefore they cannot be our ancestors. However, "it is clear," he says, "that men were first produced within fishes, and nourished like the mud-fish; and, when they were competent to fend for themselves, were thereupon cast on shore and took to the land." Anaximander is said to have reasoned that since sharks do show tenderness to their young, they were either our ancestors or our foster-parents. This fancy, however, may have been fabricated by Anaximander's later scholarly enemies. But his views seem, in part, to have departed from empirical observations of biological changes (tadpole to frog, chrysalis to

31

butterfly) and he does seem to have had a genuinely evolutionary notion.

Empedocles of Agrigentum (born 496 B.C.) gives a special account of living things as due to a process of evolution. While there is much that is fanciful and indeed mystical in Empedocles, he did a) emphasize man's relation to other living things; and b) enunciate, in a measure, the principle of natural selection. Empedocles dealt only with the adaptation of the complete organism. Democritus was interested in the functions of its parts. Anaxagoras, Archelaus, and Aristotle also adumbrated aspects of biological evolution, and all have been acclaimed as in some sense forerunners of Darwin. Aristotle holds an orthogenetic point of view but asserts that the elimination of the unfit is equally operative in the present:

> Whenever then all the parts came about just what they would have been if they had come to be for an end, such things survived, being organized spontaneously in a fitting way; whereas those which grew otherwise perished and continued to perish, as Empedocles says (*Physics*, II, 198b, 29 f.)

All of the thinkers I have mentioned made the same sort of distinction as Anaximander between the short-lived, infusorian, and almost amorphous fauna of sun-warmed water or slime and the higher orders of thinking vertebrates, among whom Man stands merely as an exceptionally rational species. According to the important line of Greek thought which started with the Ionian naturalists, there is no question of a special creation of Man. Men are part of nature and evolved within nature. By the Hippocratean period there was already an almost Darwinian outlook on the animal kingdom and a knowledge of comparative anatomy which, after the end of classical antiquity, was not attained again until the Renaissance. There were a number of remarkable anticipations such as Anaxagoras' stressing the linkages between human hands, tool-making, intelligence, and culture. Diogenes of Apollonia made much of the advantages of human erect posture—his reasons are not convincing, but the point is good. Anaxagoras and Diogenes were criticized by Aristotle on teleological grounds yet modern anthropology agrees with them on the crucial importance of hands and posture in human evolution.

On cultural evolution, Empedocles, like Hesiod, assumes degeneration from a Golden Age. Hesiod's stages are basically archaeological, characterized by their type artifacts. And his observation that primitive man was a non-agricultural forest dweller who subsisted on gathering is decent anthropological inference. Yet Hesiod depicts cultural devolution rather than evolution. Democritus, on the other hand, seems to have sketched a theory of gradual progress. The earliest stages of human civilization were imitated from the lower animals. Languages are purely conventional (*nomos*) rather than arising directly from nature (*physis*) as Heracleitus had argued. The Democritean position on the evolution of languages was refined by Epicurus who said that language is rooted in nature but that the varying experiences of human groups in different environments give rise to the development of diverse vocabularies and grammars. The fullest naturalistic account of cultural evolution in antiquity is to be found, of course, in Lucretius, but this is presumably based upon Greek sources. Herodotus discusses more than once the evolution of customs and also their independent invention. Language and culture can change under stress of circumstances in just the same way as physique; and therefrom follows the possibility of the transmission of culture. Herodotus indeed gives preference to diffusion. Athenian women have borrowed first the Dorian and then the Carian dress. Persian civilization derives much from Media and Egypt. The Colchians, Syrians, and Phoenicians took the custom of circumcision from Egypt. The *Prometheus* of Aeschylus is in its way an account of cultural evolution with the discovery of numbers as the masterpiece of civilizing wisdom. Thucydides says specifically that survivals of earlier cultures may be detected in higher civilizations; and, "ancient Greeks once resembled the present barbarians in their manner of life" (I, 5-7). Plato may borrow from Thucydides when he says: "It is not long since the Greeks held the opinion (still retained by most of the barbarians) that a naked man is an indecent and laughable sight" (*Republic,* 452 C). Aristotle's *Politics* assumes that the evolved cultures derive from the simpler.

The Greeks did not have a well-defined concept of biological race. Only at the individual level was biology significant. To Aristotle and to others there were "natural" slaves. But, so far as groups were concerned, the Greeks were quite sophisticated in deprecating the value of phenotypical criteria. They were curious about beardlessness and androgyny in certain populations, but their explanations tended to be environmental or cultural. Herodotus says that physique "comes to nothing, for there are others who have dark skin and curly hair." Color was no stigma to the Greeks, for they attributed color differences quite casually to climate and geography. Men were not classified as white or black but as free or servile. Frequently the distinction between "Greeks" and "Barbarians" is often misinterpreted. Here I would even venture to take slight issue with my learned friend, Professor Robinson, in his excellent book: *Athens in the Age of Pericles* (1959). Though Greeks were immensely proud of being Greek, "Barbarians" designates in the first instance just those who do not speak Greek—it is in no sense a "racial" category.

The proof lies in the fact that, as Herodotus says, barbarians like the Pelasgians and the Lelegians can *become* Hellenes. Thucydides tells us that Hellenism is acquired by contact with and imitation of a genuine Hellene. And we sometimes forget that the Greeks often praised and admired the "Barbarians." The opening sentence in Herodotus speaks of "the great and wonderful actions of the Greeks *and of* the Barbarians." Herodotus praises the bravery of the Persians at Plataea. Aeschylus attributed the Persian defeat not to the degeneracy of the people but to the overweening pride of Xerxes. The Greeks constantly speak of the Egyptians with respect. Plato, in the *Laws,* proposes borrowing from "Barbarian" cultures whatever is useful. Later, Eratosthenes says that groups should only be distinguished by their moral qualities, not their physical.

Let us come, finally, to theory of culture. We have already seen that Herodotus had grasped what today we call "the principle of cultural relativity." As a matter of fact there is a Greek text about a century earlier which gives a clear statement of this principle. Xenophanes, born in 560 B.C., wrote:

Yes, and if oxen and horses or lions had hands, and could paint with their hands, and produce works of art as men do, horses would paint the forms of the gods like horses, and oxen like oxen, and make their bodies in the image of their several kinds. . . . The Ethiopians make their gods black and snub-nosed; the Thracians say theirs have blue eyes and red hair.

And the inquiry into the interdependence between personal characteristics of a people and their culture and environment which in contemporary anthropology goes under the rubric of "culture and personality studies" is explicitly foreshadowed in the Hippocratean corpus:

35

The same reasoning applies also to character. In such a climate arise wildness, unsociability, and spirit. For the frequent shocks to the mind impart wildness, destroying tameness and gentleness. For this reason, I think, Europeans are also more courageous than Asiatics. For uniformity engenders slackness, while variation fosters endurance in both body and soul; rest and slackness are food for cowardice, endurance and exertion for bravery. Wherefore Europeans are more warlike, and also because of their institutions, not being under kings as are Asiatics. For, as I said above, where there are kings, there must be the greatest cowards. For men's souls are enslaved, they refuse to run risks readily and recklessly to increase the power of somebody else. But independent people, taking risks on their own behalf and not on behalf of others, are willing and eager to go into danger, for they themselves enjoy the prize of victory. So institutions contribute a great deal to the formation of courageousness.

There is no term in Greek which covers a conceptual terrain precisely equivalent to the concept of culture in the technical anthropological sense. *Ethos* or its plural *ethea* does designate "the ways of men" in Hesiod and thereafter. *Ethos* is contrasted with biological heredity. Thus Isocrates says:

Our city has caused the name of Greeks to appear no longer a sign of blood but of mind; it is those who share our culture who are called Greeks rather than those who share our blood.

Perhaps *nomos* is the closest, though *tropos* is also close as used sometimes by Pindar and other authors and in a line from Euripides' *Iphigenia in Aulis* which may properly be translated as, "Different cultures have different codes of behavior." In any event it will be worthwhile to follow out a little the controversy over *nomos* and *physis* in the fifth and fourth centuries, a controversy strangely reminiscent of that over "nature and nurture" in our nineteenth century.

First, let me say something about "theory" as I intend its meaning here. One must distinguish "theory" as abstractly constructed and deductively formulated from "speculation" whether sheer fantasy or an *ad hoc* hypothesis arising out of observation. In the anthropological or quasi-anthropological materials that have been reviewed the derivation of human-kind from stones or trees represents a speculation of the first class, presumably referable to images that animals of a certain biological type living in comparable situations produce recurrently from the unconscious. Hippocrates' attempt to link the beardlessness of wealthy Scythians with their equestrian habits is a case of an *ad hoc* explanation departing from observed data. But when we come to certain of the materials on biological evolution we are in a truly theoretical realm, for they take off from generalized and abstract premises: the continuity of all living things; gradual development, and the like.

Werner Jaeger in *Paideia* asks why a man-centered people like the Greeks approached the question of human nature systematically only after they had worked out a science of physical nature and gives this answer:

> The Greeks did not think of human nature as a theoretical problem until, by studying the external world, especially through medicine and mathematics, they had established an exact technique on which to begin a study of the inner nature of man . . . the Greek spirit, trained to think of the external cosmos as governed by fixed laws, searches for the inner laws that govern the soul, and at last discovers an objective view of the internal cosmos. . . . Thus in the fact that the philosophy of the soul was preceded by the philosophy of nature, there is a deep historical meaning which comes out when we study the history of culture as a whole (1939, pp. 150-151).

It was in the ancient Greek science of Ionia, Sicily, and Abdera that, for the first time, men on this earth arrived at a conception of man and nature in which every event and thing is thought of as intellectually known only when it is embedded in an abstractly constructed, deductively formu-

37

lated theory. Physical and human phenomena were seen as instances of universal laws as well as inductively given generalizations. "There are two things that one would rightly attribute to Socrates," says Aristotle, "inductive reasoning and universal definition." In fact, both are much earlier—going back to Ionian science—even though formulated less explicitly and with less refinement. The generality is the important "new" feature. As Professor Robinson says in discussing sculpture, the Greeks were more interested in Man than in men.

The story of *physis* and *nomos* is long and complicated, and I must necessarily oversimplify. By the fifth century Athenian thinkers were protesting that if *physis* (nature) accounted for everything there was no legitimate place for moral codes. The Sophists contrasted the uniformities of nature with the diversities of social custom, and regarded the latter as more or less arbitrary conventions which, since they were humanly created, could be humanly changed. Protagoras seems to have held that a society by rational critique of its culture, by "modernizing its *nomos*," could bring about the best of all possible worlds. There has been much discussion of Protagoras' *anthropos, metron panton.* Plato and many others took it to mean "man is the measure or criterion of all things." Aristotle says this is an absurd interpretation. Untersteiner argues that *metron* means "master," and we would then have:

Man is the master of all things, of the things that are in-so-far as they are, and of the things that are not in-so-far as they are not.

At any rate, Protagoras and others held a view which I do not think was stated categorically in the post-Greek Western world until Vico in the eighteenth century said, "Surely the social world is the work of man."

38

In the Platonic dialogue of his name, Protagoras maintains that *arete* (virtue) can be taught—not so much, however, by formal teaching as by what anthropologists call "social control." For Socrates, on the other hand, *arete* is, or should be, *episteme,*—organized knowledge (*Wissenschaft*). Plato attempted to harmonize nature and culture. Both *paideia* and *politeia* are to be based upon a scientific knowledge of nature. Man attains his true good and proper measure of perfection through insight into the abiding forms which are revealed through a study of mathematical science and dialectical synthesis. To deny—as Plato did—that man is the universal measure still leaves open the question: how is one to determine the universal nature of man? This question, according to Plato, could not be answered without a dialectical knowledge of nature as a whole. Though the ontological nature of the individual is logically prior to any given social order, Plato presents us in the *Republic* with the thesis of contemporary psychological anthropology: the culture of a given society is integrated about a selected personality type. The individual who participates in a given cultural configuration takes on the social character which is exemplified in that society as a whole.

The *Republic* can be considered as much an anthropological essay on the nature of man as a set of blueprints for the ideal state. Plato assumes the natural inequality of men, leading to the economic division of labor and to the selection and breeding and education of those most nearly adequate to govern. Instead of seeing with the Sophists a necessary conflict between *physis* and *nomos,* he undertook to show (*Republic, Gorgias, Laws*) that there is a *nomos,* a principle of development and control, in the *physis* of man, within the natural law of the cosmos. This means that human nature, despite hereditary differences, has a certain general uniformity (which justifies the Platonic psychological analysis), but that man's full nature is achieved only as it is formed by society; he is a composite of heredity and environment and individuality but is absolutely determined by none of them. The perfect balance of factors is imaginable only in a perfect society; in any existing society even the finest natural capacity (*physis*) fails to find its appropriate nurture (*trophe*) or is actually corrupted by it and the more grievously corrupted, the greater its original promise. Thus, under the horticultural figure of nature and nurture, Plato reckons with the problem that anthropologists raise today in terms of man and culture. Professor William Greene has written (1953, p. 49): "It almost seems as if the latest trend in modern anthropology is a tacit return to Platonism." I am inclined to agree with him so far as the following fundamental points are concerned:

1. The existence of a general or "raw" human nature.
2. Cultural relativity does not lead to moral nihilism, to a complete denial of ethical absolutes, but rather constitutes a comparative and scientific method of discovering these absolutes.
3. A middle term (culture) must be interposed between "nature" and the individual.

Aristotle on the nature of man seems to me less internally consistent and less satisfying than Plato. He often accepts the postulate of the uniformity of nature and the relativity of culture. Fire, he says, burns both here and in Persia, whereas Greek manners are different from the Persian. On the other hand, in the *De Interpretatione* (16a, 5) he points out that though men have different languages and forms of writing, yet the mental states which these symbolize are the same for all, as are the things for which they stand. The emphasis is on the unity and permanence of the mental states and that to which they correspond in the objective world. All men have minds which are alike *in reality* but *in appearance* the identity is concealed behind a screen of difference. This I find good anthropology. In Aristotle's thought, he often seems to be saying—as Heracleitus expressly did—that the universals are precisely the residual identities existing among individuals when their differences are subtracted. But Aristotle's discussion in the *Nicomachean Ethics* and its sequel, the *Politics,* strikes me as confusing. Nature is uniform, though sometimes chance interferes. Man's superiority to the beasts lies in his ability to guide himself by reason rather than relying on nature and habit. Aristotle says, "Men do many things contrary to habit and nature, if they should be persuaded by their reason to do otherwise." He does not bother to explain how reason could persuade anyone to do something contrary to nature. There are inherent difficulties in any theory which a) believes nature to be uniform and b) absorbs man into the natural order but c) argues that he ought to be what he is not.

Obviously, Greek anthropology had severe limitations. One was inherent in the rather narrow range and variety of the cultures with which the Greeks were familiar. They barely began the development of a scientific terminology, and they had none of the methods of modern field work. The systematic collection and study of artifacts started—falteringly— only with the creation of museums in the Hellenistic Age. Leaving aside such technical matters, the broad conceptual limitation of Greek anthropology was the lack of a systematic theory of the irrational, of unconscious factors in human conduct. There were glimmerings of understanding, to be sure. Hippocrates prescribes for certain nervous diseases of young girls only marriage and pregnancy. Plato's anticipations of Freud are familiar. Aristotle had a theory of dreams and spoke of the cathartic influence of music. He and his immediate successors as directors of the Lyceum appreciated perhaps better than any other Greeks the necessity of studying the irrational if one is to gain a generalized picture of human nature. But, as Dodds writes:

> They [the Greeks] were deeply and imaginatively aware of the power, the wonder, and the peril of the Irrational. But they could describe what went on below the threshhold of consciousness only in mythological or symbolic language; they had no instrument for understanding it, still less for controlling it; and in the Hellenistic Age too many of them made the fatal mistake of thinking they could ignore it (1951, p. 254).

And yet the wonder to me is that they went so far, so early. The best of the Greeks saw man as a part of nature and to be naturalistically understood. They recognized that man was an animal, and that his development had to be investigated in the light of the evolution of living things generally. Some of the Greeks more than half formulated the principle of natural selection. On the other hand, they did not fall into the error of biological racism. They preferred the pertinence of geographical environment and culture. Human nature, both biological and psychological, was definitely plastic. Cultural diffusion played a significant role. For "culture" they did not have a focused single concept—we still do not have one that is truly sharp and clear—but they comprehended the general idea of culture better than anyone before Pufendorf in the sixteenth century. Although we find many things in their anthropology that strike us as gullible or less than partly true, still it has that quality which Plutarch ascribed to the buildings on the Acropolis: a certain flourishing freshness. Both the data and the ideas of Greek anthropology invite detailed re-examination by contemporary anthropologists and other students of man and culture.

III A Brief Grammar of Greek Culture

THIS TITLE, as announced, is much too pretentious. I was guilty of *hybris* in anticipating that I could in intermittent work over a year encompass enough of the multitudinous original sources and the still more monumental scholarly commentary upon them to give a clear and economical account of the distinctive features of Greek culture that would satisfy myself—let alone you. However, as Sir Maurice Bowra has recently written:

> It is not easy to say anything that is both new and true about the Greeks, but it is much to be desired that scholars should from time to time try to reassess their achievement in the light of modern experience and ask what in it matters most to us.

One should say something—present at least some working notes, a prolegomena.

To begin with, there are some theoretical premises. The term "grammar" is used for two reasons. First, as a reminder that the conceptual scheme derives directly from recent studies of the linguistic aspects of cultures. Second, because I assume that as in a grammar or in a phonological system there are a comparatively small number of basic principles, the influence of which may be detected in wide ranges of content. As the British biologist, J. Z. Young, has recently written: "Each human society usually has some central model as the canon of its system" (1951, p. 153). Students of cultures must do as the linguists have done and identify the significant structure points which define the essential character of each culture. The function of linguistic grammar is to control the freedom of words so that there is no needless congestion of communication traffic. The "grammar" of each culture likewise provides the necessary minimum of orderliness. All grammars limit freedom and control choices. The anthropologist must be interested in the total language, leaving the dialects to the historians and perhaps the pyschologists. In the light of some empirical inquiries carried out over the past decade, it is likely that the distinctive essence of each culture could be defined fairly well if one were able to isolate between ten and twenty thematic principles which in their hierarchical combinations would characterize the structure of that culture.

A second assumption is that the key to cultural structure in this sense rests largely in three related sets of data:

1) The cultural premises about "the nature of things."
2) Cultural value-emphases.
3) Certain of the distinctive categories of the culture.

By the latter I mean those concepts of which Carl Becker has written in *The Heavenly City of the Eighteenth Century Philosophers:*

If we would discover the little backstairs door that for any age serves as the secret entranceway to knowledge, we will do well to look for certain unobtrusive words with uncertain meanings that are permitted to slip off the tongue or the pen without fear and without research; words which, having from constant repetition lost their metaphorical significance, are unconsciously mistaken for objective realities. . . . In each age these magic words have their entrances and their exits (1935, p. 47).

These ideas are not necessarily peculiar to the culture in question but they are designated by words that are very difficult to translate into other languages (in Greek, *hamartia, moira, sophrosyne,* for example).

The examination of such concepts can be extremely instructive, but in the present context I shall deal with them mainly to elucidate the existential and evaluative postulates of Greek culture, for I believe these postulates to be the implicit framework of the distinctive categories. I shall give particular attention to the value-emphases because I am convinced that if the cardinal fact about cultures is their selectivity of means and modes and goals from the great variety of possibilities that are open in "the objective world," then the understanding of this patterned selectivity comes most easily and most fully from a grasp of the core values of the culture. This is not to say that the existential premises are unimportant. Far from it. Choice of values occurs only within the realm of what is deemed possible by the participants in the culture, and this realm is defined by beliefs about the nature of things.

First, it seems necessary to say something about the conception of values used here. In the broadest sense, behavioral scientists may usefully think of values as abstract and perduring standards which are held by an individual and/or a specified group to transcend the impulses of the moment and ephemeral situations. From the psychological point of view, a value may be defined as that aspect of motivation which is referable to standards, personal or cultural, that do not arise solely out of an immediate situation and the satisfaction of needs and primary drives. Concretely, of course, values are always manifested in the verbal and motor behavior of individuals—including what is *not* said and *not* done. There are research purposes for which it is necessary to focus upon personal values as such, though such personal values are ordinarily no more than the idiosyncratic variants of values which may, by abstraction, be attributed to a group or to a culture or subculture. However, not everything culturally valued constitutes a value in the meaning intended but only those principles on the highest level of generality from which more specific norms and acts of valuation can be derived. Henceforth I shall be dealing solely with cultural values in this sense.

A value is a selective orientation toward experience, implying deep commitment or repudiation, which influences the ordering of "choices" between possible alternatives in action. These orientations may be cognitive and expressed verbally or merely inferable from recurrent trends in behavior. (One merit of the study of values by behavioral scientists is that values are drawn out into the realm of the explicit.) A value, though conditioned by biological and social necessity, is in its particular form arbitrary and conventional. Values are related to and dependent upon nature, but they are not "in nature" in the same fashion as, for instance, mass and energy. Specifically cultural values (both *seriatim* and even more in culturally specific combinations) contribute as much to cultural definitions of the situation as do each culture's existential beliefs.

Behavior oriented by a value or by values constitutes one class of preferential behavior. But such behavior belongs to the category regarded as "desirable" or "undesirable" by the group with which the individual identifies—not to that of acts which a person simply desires or does not desire. With values there is always the implication of conflict or tension. Mere desiring does not instate a value; the desires have, as it were, to be criticized and compared. Sometimes, to be sure, the two categories of desired and desirable merge in the life experience of wise or fortunate individuals. A saying is attributed to Confucius: "In my old age I found that I had to do what I wanted to do and wanted to do what I had to do." Nevertheless, both introspection and observation tell us forcefully that the areas of the desirable and the desired are not always—or even often —coextensive.

This circumstance sometimes escapes behavioral scientists. When I talk to clinical psychologists they frequently say, "Oh, yes, I know what you mean by 'value.' It is what we call 'need' or 'cathexis.'" And the experimental psychologists will similarly remark, "That is what we refer to as 'drive strength.'" If this equation of concepts were adequate to our data, we should—on the principle of Occam's razor—simply drop the term, "value." Yet it is an induction from ordinary experience that, on occasion, all of us behave in ways that go contrary, in whole or in part, to our "wants" or "desires" as they arise in the biological organism at that moment. The existence of the value-element may transform the desired into the not-desired or the ambivalently desired. Disvalued activity is frequently cathected. A cathexis is an impulse. A value or values restrain or canalize impulses in terms of what a group has defined as wider or more enduring goods.

Values, then, are images formulating positive or negative action commitments, a set of hierarchically ordered prescriptions and proscriptions. Without a hierarchy of values human behavior could be described by a list of instincts and a probabilistic calculus. Human life would become a sequence of reactions to unconfigurated stimuli. Values are standards which complicate the individual's satisfactions of his immediate wishes and needs. They take distinctive forms in different cultures, tend to persist tenaciously through time, and are not mere random outcomes of conflicting human desires.

Linguists in their elegant analyses of one aspect of culture have found it extremely useful to set up a series of distinctive contrasts or oppositions, usually binary, which serve to identify each separate phoneme (sound class distinctive in that language). A "lump" or "bundle" of such "distinctive features" defines a phoneme. In its simplest form, the process is like a specialized version of the "twenty questions game." Thus one may ask, "Is the phoneme vocalic? Yes or no?" In Russian, eleven such questions will identify each phoneme uniquely. In the French phonemic system, the binary oppositions are the following: vowel-consonant, nasal-oral, saturated-diluted, grave-acute, tense-lax, and continuous-intercepted. While the particular principles or distinctive features and their combinations vary from one phonemic system to another, a total list of the oppositions utilized in known languages would not exceed twenty, and only some dozen have been identified.

There are grounds for supposing that a similar approach will yield good results with other aspects of culture, including cultural values. Human nature and the human situation are such that there are some fundamental questions of value upon which all cultures have taken a position, explicit or implicit. As in the case of language, the foci or structure-points are largely supplied by the limits and potentialities given by the physical world, human biology, and social requirements. With language, the properties of sound waves, the anatomy and physiology of the speech organs, and social (communicative) needs constrain the range of variation. With values, such unavoidable facts as dependence upon the external environment, birth and death, and social relatedness make value "choices" in these areas inescapable. Nor here again is the range of loci for selection or indeed of possible selections at each locus unconstrained. Just as all phonemic systems include nasals, stops, and sibilants, so all value systems place their weightings, for instance, on the desirable relations to nature, other individuals, and the self within a describable set of alternatives. The entities of value-culture do not have the all-or-none character of a simple physical event like the phonemes found in language culture. Rather, they seem to have the character of weightings or emphases that are, on the whole, dominant in the culture. Even here there are parallels. A language or a phonemic system is, after all, a high order abstraction. Concretely, each person's speech is an idiodialect, and even this varies through time and between situations. Similarly, some individuals or groups may accept the variant rather than the dominant cultural values. They may reject some or many of the core values. To those values, whether dominant or variant, that they do accept each individual gives an interpretation and a coloring that is more or less private. It nevertheless remains meaningful to abstract common elements both in language and in values.

This is what I shall attempt for Greek culture. I shall be concerned with what Heracleitus considered "the real": that which overlaps between different minds. We are all aware that between Homer and Aristotle there were major shifts in Greek thought and in Greek values. Nevertheless, there remained much continuity. Of any culture we must say, *Plus ça change, plus c'est la même chose.* Otherwise we should not be dealing with a genuine culture. Whenever there are significant discontinuities—and especially in the value structure—we must speak of another culture. But from Graeco-Roman antiquity to the present day, the way of life of the Greeks from Homer until at least the Hellenistic period has been recognized as an entity in spite of all the internal variations. Here I want to talk about the dominant and, on the whole, the persistent. For other purposes, the variant—as between period and period, region and region, author and author—might well claim our interest.

In recent years my students and I have done a number of trial runs in constructing cultural profiles according to a set of binary oppositions. Incidentally, this approach—like so many other logical techniques—goes back to the Greeks, to the Heracleitean "complementarity of opposites" and to the *dissoi logoi,* the "two-fold arguments" of Parmenides and Protagoras. The particular contrasts used were obtained in the first instance from the study of the philosophical and anthropological literature and then modified through a series of successive approximations as a consequence of our empirical experience. The ontological status of these pairs is not that of true dichotomies but rather that of bi-polar dimensions. The two-feature oppositions are not so constituted that one empirically excludes the presence of the other. It is rather a question of dominance of emphasis. This is a system of priorities— not of all-or-none categories. In contrast to Wittgenstein's "atomic propositions" where one must say either "yes" or "no," here the rater decides "the weight falls more this way than that way." In one instance, with the Greek materials, we were forced to conclude that the weight was about evenly balanced. Time will not permit me to deal with all of the thirteen pairs with which my collaborators and I have been working. I can only illustrate with some of the contrasts I feel to be especially significant in the Greek case.

"Determinate" vs. "Indeterminate." This contrast hinges upon the priority given to orderliness (lawfulness) in the universe as opposed to chance or divine caprice. Here Greek culture seems to me clearly on the "determinate" polarity. Jocasta could say, "chance rules our lives." Aristotle reluctantly admitted but patently did not like a category of indeterminate events. But not until Hellenistic times, as Dodds remarks, did the cults of divinities of chance attain widespread popularity. Many scholars have found either in the Ionian philosopher-physicists or in the tragedians the first statement of the scien-

tific view: a lawful and orderly world. Actually, even to Homer there were no "accidents." For him, as for Freud, everything is somehow determined. In later Greek culture there are two kinds of determinism, though often blended in the concrete instance. On the one hand, there is the Aeschylean "entangled in the impassable net of *ate*." On the other, the naturalistic regularities of the Ionians. (As Dodds observes, the leading Ionians were freer of supernaturalism than the leading Athenians of Aeschylus' day.) But both are forms of the "remorseless working out of things."

"Unitary" vs. "Pluralistic." Is the world, including human life, thought of as a single manifold or as segmented into two or more spheres in which different principles prevail? At first glance this contrast might appear to be a special case of the first. Certainly it would seem logically probable that the unitary emphasis would be likely to be found where the deterministic emphasis dominates. But there are innumerable instances of "mechanistic" cultures exhibiting the familiar dualisms of "sacred and profane," "mind and body," not merely as categories of a larger whole but as altogether separate realms governed by distinct "laws" and with one construed as more permanent and superior to the other.

I confess to considerably less than full confidence of my assessment of the pertinent Greek evidence on this point. One can argue that "mortal"-"immortal" constitutes a clear and sharp sundering of realms. "Know Thyself" did originally mean: "remember that you are a mortal" and one can muster massive additional documentation along the same line. And yet it strikes me, as an anthropologist, that the Greek barrier between the human and the divine categories was far more permeable than in most cultures with which I am familiar. As Sophocles says:

Great fame it is
To share the lot of those equal to gods
In life, and thereafter in death. (*Antigone,* 836-838.)

The gods were not only anthropomorphic. In all except a few particulars they talked and reasoned and behaved like human beings. Moreover, they constantly entered the human sphere and mortals the divine. There is a long list of beings whose status is so equivocal that modern students have spoken of them as "demi-gods." On balance, I would maintain that the weight falls rather definitely on the "unitary" pole. Both the Ionian and the Sicilian philosophers sought with desperate conviction for a single principle or essence whether water or fire or number from which all phenomena finally derived. Heracleitus' "everything changes; nothing remains" is, after all, a declaration of endless continuity and his "harmony in contrariety, as in the case of the flute and the lyre," an affirmation of unity. His cosmos was none the less a unity for being full of tensions. Democritus, as we all know, reduced the unspeakably rich manifold of events to ultimate particles and purely geometrical images. And one of the most beautiful and brilliant of the fragments denies in moving fashion *any* duality between the phenomenological world and the final scientific reality:

Ostensibly there is sweetness, ostensibly bitterness, actually only atoms and the void. *To which the senses retort:* Poor intellect, do you hope to defeat us while from us you borrow your evidence? Your victory is your defeat.

One simply cannot put it more briefly and clearly. No, I think the Greeks who believed in ineluctable laws, both supernatural and natural, had a profoundly unitary conception of the universe and experience in it.

The "Human" vs. the "Supernatural." The evidence is overwhelming that the Greek emphasis was upon man. The Jews took righteousness as the supreme virtue. The Christians took the pleasing of God as the highest good. Not so the Greeks. As Saint Paul remarked, "Christ seems to the Greeks to be foolishness, for they seek after wisdom" (a human quality). A word meaning "love of God" does not even appear in the Greek language until the third century.

In other cultures the emphasis upon the supernatural is negative—i.e. fear of supernatural forces. This note is by no means totally absent from Greek culture but it is often counter-balanced by proud defiance, by the assertion that human beings can be victorious even in their defeat at the hands of malignant supernatural powers.

None of this is intended to suggest that religion was insignificant in Greece. I do suggest that religious belief and practice were thought of as for the benefit of man rather than for the benefit of the gods. I think we may take it that the more personal and more profound religious needs of the Greeks found their full satisfaction in the mysteries of Eleusis and Samothrace, or in the Dionysiac, Orphic, and Pythagorean sects. As for the official and public cults, they were intended to hold the social fabric firm. One should not commit open religious transgressions, and one ought to participate in the rites of the official cult. Faith was not a test. There were no heretics and dissenters. Foreigners were perfectly free to worship their own deities by their own rituals. If a *Greek* denied the *existence* of the Greek gods, this could be taken as at least a pretext for social sanction. But note that most of the trials which we know to have taken place occurred during a thirty-year span beginning with the Peloponnesian War—a period when the solidarity of Athenian society was manifestly threatened. And note that the banishment of Anaxagoras was

designed to strike at Pericles, and that the execution of Socrates was more motivated by socio-political than by strictly
religious ends.

I do not want to seem to claim too much here. I am quite
aware that Hesiod, Pindar, and other writers seem to have
been very devout. I know that Plato in the *Laws* (716 c) said that
"the measure of all things is God." But I also recall that in the
Timaeus Plato observed that "the great God" is hard to find
and impossible to explain to the masses. One can certainly
document the view that the Greeks claimed that gods and men
live in a single world, belong ultimately to a single race, and
that what makes man what he is at his best comes from the
gods. Perhaps Professor Hadas is right in his recent book,
Humanism, when he maintains that the Greeks worked out a
tenable system for the relations of gods and men, and through
this were able to give human beings their own purpose and
their own dignity in following it.

Most Greeks—surely in the earlier centuries—believed in
the power of the gods. This is unarguable. I am certain that
Aeschylus spoke for the culture of his epoch when he says in
the *Suppliants:* "with Zeus alone, thought, word, and deed are
one." Yet, however the divine and its power be envisaged, the
accent is forever upon man. This is reflected in Socrates' light-
hearted description of the cosmos as having been created for
man's delight. It shines to give man light; the moon and the
stars mark the hours and seasons for his benefit. To an objector
who remarks that the animals also enjoy these benefits, Socrates retorts that the animals have also been created for the
service of man. In a different way but equally it is reflected in
fearless human challenges to the gods. Remember this is very
early in the cultural history of mankind. I know of no comparable culture where there is so much open back-talk to the

deities and to conventional religion. I have quoted Xenophanes and Heracleitus. One can also instance the *Zeu,
thaumadzute* of Theognis and Herodotus: "The Hellenes tell
many things without proper examination; among them is the
silly myth they tell about Heracles." Thucydides says of the
period of the plague, "as to supplications in temples, inquiries
of oracles, and the like, they were utterly useless." From a later
time one could mention Lucian's catechism of Zeus.

But I think it needless to extend this catalogue unduly. I
would rest my case for this point upon the Greek statements
on "happiness" which I have been collecting for some years.
One sometimes encounters reference to happiness as proceeding from the gods. Solon in his "Prayer to the Muses" says:
"Let me at all times obtain good fortune from the blessed gods
and enjoy honorable repute among men." But note the
juxtaposition of the second clause! Techomachus in the *Economics* of Xenophon reckons among subjects of prayer: health,
bodily strength, good repute in the city, kindly relations with
friends, safety in war, increase of wealth. But note that every
blessing invoked is mortal and secular! Most of the definitions
I have found are wholly humanistic. The description is entirely
in terms of the human condition rather than in terms of happiness being conceived in terms of communion with the deities,
pleasing the gods, or the joys of an after-life. Solon, as quoted
by Herodotus, says that the man "who may rightly be termed
happy" is "whole of limb, a stranger to disease, free from mis-
fortune, happy in his children, and comely to look upon."
Aristotle's "happiness" is altogether worldly:

Prosperity combined with virtue; or independence of life; or that
existence which, being safe, is pleasantest; or a flourishing state of
prosperity and of body, with the faculty of guarding and producing
this; for it may be said that all men allow happiness to be one or
more of these things. If then happiness is this sort of thing, these

must be parts of it; good birth, the possession of many friends, wealth, the possession of good children, the possession of many children, a happy old age; further the excellence of the body as health, beauty, strength, great stature, athletic power; also good repute, honor, good fortune, virtue. For a man would then be most independent, if he possessed both the personal and the external goods, since besides these are no others (*Rhetoric,* 1360 B; tr. Jebb).

"Evil" vs. "Good." Cultures ordinarily attribute to inanimate nature, to supernatural beings, and to human nature properties that are positively or negatively toned. Nature is threatening or beneficent; the supernaturals may or may not be effectively propitiated; human nature is basically good or evil. To be sure, the judgments usually come in mixed or qualified form, but frequently one polarity or the other stands out. It seems definitely so in the Greek case. In spite of all the gusto of Greek life, there is a persistent note of the melancholy of mortality, of fear of indifference or evil in the supernatural world, of evil in other human beings and hence suspicion of their motives—as Professor Robinson and others have pointed out. One need only recall a few familiar but representative quotations:

"It were best never to have been born" (Sophocles, *Oedipus at Colonus*).
"Count no man happy" (Sophocles, *Oedipus the King*).
"For oftentimes God gives men a gleam of happiness and then plunges them into ruin" (Herodotus).
"All human destiny is full of the fear and the peril that good fortune may be followed by evil. He who stands clear of trouble should beware of dangers; and when a man lives at ease, then it is that he should look most closely to his life, lest ruin come upon it by stealth" (Sophocles, *Philoctetes*).
"So then neither can God, since he is good, be the cause of everything as the many say, but for man he is the cause of a few things but of many he is not the cause. For good things are far fewer with us than evil and it is God and no one else that we must take to be

the cause of the good, but for the evil we must find some other cause, but not God" (Plato, *Republic*).

It seems that the Greek notion could be summed up thus: even if the framework within which we order our lives is roughly calculated to give us some prospect of happiness, even if divine justice be *ultimately* meted out, clearly this is a world in which the innocent often suffer and the wicked often prosper. At best, justice and law are abstract and have no respect for particular individuals who, moreover, are partly at the mercy of force and of chance. And, so far as the supernatural world is concerned, Cedric Whitman convincingly—to me, at least— argues that Sophocles drew the bitter implication that what was believed of the gods and what showed itself in their active dealings with men was so incongruent that the world is indeed full of evil and tragedy, a world not subject to simple moral rules. Men may live nobly to no ultimate purpose.

"Individual" vs. "Group." The Greeks themselves and all observers and analysts of Greek culture from the earliest times to the present have been almost unanimous that in the final analysis it was the individual who counted. Of course, the person had duties to family, to lineage, to deme and tribe, and in the later centuries to the *polis*. And there were sanctions, religious and secular, imposed upon those who shirked their responsibilities. It may be conceded that there is a marked difference between the fifth and fourth centuries as regards individualism and loyalty to the state. And there are variations between other periods. But only reluctantly for the most part did the Greek individual see himself as a means to the end of some collectivity. There is plenty of individualism—indeed of exhibitionistic individualism—in Homer. And if the *Oresteia* be a paean to the triumph of the abstract justice of the *polis* over the tribal custom of an eye for an eye and a tooth for a

tooth, the *Antigone* is a magnificent assertion that individuals have the duty to assert such rights even against duly constituted authority. In the *Philebus* (60 B) Socrates praises *autarky,* self-sufficiency, as the *finis bonorum,* and the same view is attributed to Antisthenes and to many Epicurean and Stoic philosophers. Aristotle—at least in the *Politics*—rejects this position on the ground that it would make men asocial and this would be contrary to their nature. But Aristotle was aiming at political stability in and after a time of confusion. Surely it is indisputable that the dominant Greek stand was that the state exists for the individual rather than the reverse. Many Greeks went far beyond *autarky* and spoke of *authadeia,* that special quality of self-willed independence which keeps a man from yielding to his fate and makes him talk harshly and proudly. *Authadeia* is the outstanding quality of Agamemnon, Clytemnestra, Ajax, Prometheus, Antigone, and countless other tragic figures.

"Self" vs. "Other." This dichotomy refers to the relative emphasis placed upon egoism and altruism. Here the "other" consists in other individuals rather than in various solidary collectivities. For example, loyalty and devotion—at some expense to the interests of the self—are enjoined toward wife, children, and other relatives as persons rather than as a family entity. Or, in other cultures, the emphasis may be directed primarily toward friends or occupational or ritual associates or to a god or gods. In any case the needs of the self are placed as high or low in reference to the needs of others (*as individual personalities*). There is no hesitation in placing the Greeks on the "self" dimension. Loyalty to friends and leaders and often to parents and other relatives is recorded but one has to strain for examples like the Spartan and Theban pairs or Sappho for indications of romantic or self-effacing attachment. Even Sappho's

love appears quite self-centered. And the band at Thermopylae whose funeral monument says, "Go, tell the Spartans, thou that passest by, that here obedient to their laws we lie," were sacrificing themselves for the state rather than for their individual friends. In spite of the *Symposium,* Greek friendship was mainly interested rather than disinterested: "Drink with me, be young with me, wear garlands with me." And repeatedly in response to the question "why have children?" one gets the statement: "To feed my old age." Altruism in the Christian sense is hard to find in Greek culture.

"Free" vs. "Bound." This contrast is clearly related to but by no means precisely co-extensive with the "determinate"-"indeterminate" polarity. Among other things, this pair refers exclusively to the human sphere. Can the individual, as argued in the *Republic,* make a choice between the lives he will lead? To what extent is he morally responsible for his acts? The evidence in the Greek case is admittedly complex but to dismiss the matter with the frequently expressed view that the dominant Greek view of life placed man wholly at the mercy of inexorable necessity or "fate" is quite wrong. Greene in his book, *Moira,* has summarized the traditional conception about as follows. Human error (*hamartia*) leads to an inevitable sequence. If prosperity (*olbos*) or a sense of surfeit (*koros*) instigates a man to a deed of excess (*hybris*), he will suffer retribution (*nemesis*). Indeed some of the earlier Greeks supposed that mere prosperity, apart from any misdeeds, may involve a man in such *ate* because it has aroused the jealousy (*phthonos*) of the gods. Hesiod makes *ate* the punishment of *hybris* and observes with relish that not even a nobleman can escape it.

Now it is not hard to cite passages that will support this schematization, though it is easier to do so from some authors, such as Hesiod and Herodotus, than from others. There is no doubt that the Greeks felt that there was lawful order in the universe and in human experience. They were quite clear that some things are *adunata,* "impossible." The expression, *to pepromene,* which occurs so frequently in the tragedies, designates a *fait accompli,* something which cannot be undone. In Greek writings there is recurrent praise of the manly endurance of hardship. "Endure and renounce"—even "live in obscurity" are slogans. The Greeks *were* abundantly and poignantly aware of necessity. Agamemnon's remark before he undertook the sacrifice of his daughter Iphigenia at Aulis, "I took upon myself the halter of necessity," is characteristically Greek.

All of the above is quite true. But it is not the whole story. I believe misunderstanding has resulted from the insistence, often unconscious, of modern writers to force Greek thought into the free will-determinism formula. This is un-Greek. I do not believe any classical Greek ever thought in precisely those terms. In any event, the so-called problem seems to me a bogus one except possibly as regards pure metaphysics. From the psychological point of view, the propositions "I can make choices" and "I feel I have to operate as if choice is not always an illusion" are equivalent. The most sincere and radical determinist still in his personal life has to go through the psychological agonies of "decision."

To leave the Greek position—as many scholars, in effect, have—on the line of fate or implacable necessity is to omit what is most distinctively Greek. There are three points:

1. The Greeks were convinced that they could rationally examine and decide between alternatives.
2. They were able to protest and rebel at injustice.
3. Men were morally accountable.

Plato and Aristotle are the most resplendent witnesses to the first point. I need remind you of only one quotation which is not the less glorious for being so familiar: "The unexamined life is not worth living." As Cedric Whitman says:

> The belief that any individual potentially contains valid insight into justice, divine and political, was specifically Athenian. Such insight was a kind of *arete,* the kind of *arete* peculiarly appropriate to a citizen (1951, p. 87).

It followed that the Greeks felt free to judge, to condemn evil in themselves, in others, in states. They were not so naïve as to fail to realize that this was not the best of all possible worlds. They knew quite well that the innocent often suffered and the wicked often prospered. But they retained the precious freedom of moral judgment. Prometheus is the first great rebel of literature. Adam and Eve disobeyed but did not rebel. The Greeks found in nature and in reason sufficient justification to defy man-made laws and to protest divine decrees. The Greek attitude was not dissimilar to that expressed by Edna St. Vincent Millay:

> I know.   I am aware.   I understand.
> But I do not approve and I am not reconciled.

And, as with others who have been much impressed by necessity, the recognition of the ineluctability of some events did not blind the Greeks to moral responsibility. I think the word *hamartia* has given some trouble here. Many writers, Sir Richard Livingstone among them, have leaned too heavily upon the etymology of the word—Livingstone suggests that it is a metaphor from archery and means no more than "missing the mark." He is quite right in maintaining that it is by no means an exact counter for the Jewish-Christian concept of "sin," though *hamartia* is used to translate this idea in the Greek version of the New Testament. It is true that the usage of the word in various Greek authors is sometimes puzzling. In the *Nicomachean Ethics* Aristotle divides wrong-doing

61

into three classes, one of which is *hamartia* and this is ordinarily rendered into English in this passage as "mistake" or "trifling error." But in the *Poetics* he uses the same term to refer to Oedipus' killing of his father and marriage with his mother. Here Bywater translates as "human frailty." Socrates defines *hamartia* as a kind of ignorance, but the mission of his life was to prove that such ignorance, the ignorance of values, was itself an *hamartia*.

At any rate, in a doctoral dissertation which exhaustively studies the word in context in the principal Greek authors from Homer through Menander, Henry Philipps (1933) shows that the meaning of the root (both nominal and verbal) developed from a physical sense of missing a definite mark or goal to the sense of "to err" as describing the failure to reach a mental goal. He then demonstrates that, beginning with Homer, the word is used by the same authors in two meanings: one intellectual and one moral. On the latter he points out the possible English analogy: "wrong" = "crooked" or "bent." He concludes that the Greeks did not in fact dismiss grave moral offenses as mere "errors of judgment." I have gone on at this length about *hamartia* only because so much of the argument that the Greeks did not feel morally free or morally responsible has been based on this one concept. Actually, we must conclude from many other lines of evidence that the Greeks held men to have freedom of a kind. I need cite, I think, only a few bits of such evidence. The word *aitia* (whence one of our terms for causation—aetiology) meant originally the person's accountability for his actions in the law courts. Aristophanes, in the *Clouds* and elsewhere, attacks the Sophists, because, in his view, they encouraged people to "Kick up your heels, laugh at the world, take no shame for anything." Euripides who is often (wrongly, I believe) portrayed as a sort of "decadent," has his choruses denounce those to whom *arete* and *aidos* are mere words, who "slight the law to gratify lawless impulses," who try to *eu kakourgein,* "do wrong and get away with it."

No, in several significant and distinctively Greek senses, the Greeks held man to be free rather than bound. It was not exactly the conception that some Christian thinkers have held of "free will" and "moral responsibility." Yet within the framework of lawful necessity man had some degrees of freedom and was indeed accountable. Cedric Whitman attributes these sentiments to the Greeks:

> The more we look closely for a satisfying justice in the world, the more inevitably we are driven to disillusion and to the admission that justice is with man, not the gods; that man is more responsible than he dreamed, though in a different way; and that perhaps this very quality in man is a kind of divinity (1951, p. 21).

"Discipline" vs. "Fulfillment." Roughly, this is the "Apollonian-Dionysian" contrast of Ruth Benedict. The issue is between safety and adventure, between control and expansion, between "adjustment" to the culture and internal harmony. Here I think the Greek position was about an equal weighting or a balance between the two value-qualities. Innately, the Greeks were a passionate people. They did not talk about *meden agan,* "nothing too much," because abandon had no attractions for them. Quite the contrary. They preached control because they had witnessed and experienced the perils of letting go. But the orgiastic and mystery religions—about which we know far too little—retained a prominent place in Greek culture. The participants—perhaps especially the isolated and bored Greek women—believed with Blake that "the paths of excess lead to the palaces of wisdom." Even Socrates spoke eloquently of "the blessings of madness." Even Plato agreed that all must get drunk at the Great Dionysia.

Perhaps the final ideal personality was the self-controlled

but yet daemonic man of Plato's early dialogues. The historic development, however, largely favored the polarity of discipline. We must turn once more to one of those difficult and, in my judgment, often misinterpreted words: *sophrosyne*. Professor Robinson translates it as "self-restraint." In the *Hippolytus* of Euripides it means, specifically, chastity. Only a cognate is found in Homer and that infrequently. The large Greek dictionary tells us that literally it means "of sound or whole mind" and provides the following translations: soundness of mind, moderation, good sense, prudence, discretion, self-control, temperance, chastity. The word is found first in Theognis and occurs often in Thucydides and the dramatists.

There is no doubt that in the fifth and fourth centuries there were many exhortations to *sophrosyne* in the meaning of self-restraint. Even *arete* came to mean sometimes discipline; control of the passions, of the impulse life. The Greeks often paired *sophrosyne* with *hybris* which originally meant "assault and battery" and never quite lost the overtone of physical violence. This overweening arrogance or haughtiness or rashness was condemned as overstepping proper limits of behavior and leading to just doom. But was self-restraint a positively prized Greek value or a negative caution? Mainly the latter, it would seem. One must hold entirely with Whitman when he writes of the works of Sophocles:

If we are to believe the sin-and-punishment formulae, this miracle of poetic inspiration and skill was exercised during a ninety-year lifetime in some hundred and twenty plays in order to prove to the sophisticated men of Athens a Sunday-school lesson: Be humble, be careful, and you will be happy. If that is all, it is worse than disappointing: it is vulgar. Greek mothers long before Sophocles taught their children lessons of piety and *sophrosyne*. However he may have admired these virtues, Sophocles did not write tragedy in order to teach them. In fact, though the Greeks praised these traits, and asserted them, it is far from certain how much

Sophocles or any of his countrymen really admired them (1951, p. 37).

Whitman goes on to remind us that Plato, the greatest moralist of antiquity, made *sophrosyne* the least of the car--dinal virtues and most suitable to the artisans in his polity. It is true that in the *Gorgias sophrosyne* is the basic virtue, but in the *Republic* this is rather *dikaiosune,* "justice." Plato (*Republic* 430 E) does describe *sophrosyne* as a "harmony" of temperamental tendencies but stigmatizes it as "subjugation" of the desires to reason. The principle of order and self-control is indeed affirmed, but as a subsidiary virtue.

"Now" vs. "Then." Cultures vary widely and importantly in their conceptions of time as an unbroken continuum or as segmented by a moving present or as homogeneous and instantaneous. Much could be said about the Greek concepts, and much interesting work has been done by Fraenkel and, more recently, by the Thorntons of Otago University in New Zealand. There was *chronos* which in Homer always indicated a duration and never a point but which developed in the direction of but never quite reached our principal concept. When Aristotle wanted an abstract notion, he found it necessary to speak of *to pote,* "the when." There was *kairos,* the special moment of time. There is the fact that to the Greeks it was ego who was stationary: time came up behind him and then went on ahead of time to become the future before his eyes (compare the use of *opisso*), whereas time for us is cut by a moving present.

But from the angle of values the most significant accent would seem to be that upon the here-and-now as opposed to either past or future. The Greeks overwhelmingly stressed the "now." Hesiod was an exception, and there were others. The main trend, however, is patent throughout Greek antiquity.

65

It is linked to the oppressive sense of the brevity of mortality. The Greeks felt, with Aristotle, that man is but *pneuma kai skia,* "a breath and a shadow." "Time is the father of all things," and therefore men must seize the moment before it escapes. In the words of Theognis:

> Gather my heart, oh youth, before it fly.
> Soon other men shall be, no doubt
> But I, an earthen clod in dark earth shall lie.

The message of Sophocles is that of responsibility for the present. Thucydides makes the Athenians reply to the Melians, "You are the only men who deem the future to be more certain than the present." Similar thoughts echo long after the classical period. Plutarch's prayer was "Put off old age, thou beautiful Aphrodite." Only to rare beings such as the old Oedipus could ancient years be accepted with serenity, for:

> The wise never grow old; their minds are nursed
> By living with the bold light of day.

Subject once more to the qualification that we have only fragmentary knowledge of the mystery religions, it may be said that the Greeks firmly emphasized this life rather than any hereafter. There is hardly any cult of the dead in Homer and no ghosts except for the interpolation in the eleventh book of the *Odyssey.* Some interest in what lay beyond this life is expressed in the seventh century and thereafter, but for the most part the Greeks were willing to leave the issue with the statement: "Death is evil; the gods have willed it so" (Sappho). Pericles in his famous funeral oration made no illusion whatever to immortality beyond his reference to the "memory which will live on in men's hearts."

And so I have sketched—incompletely—a profile of the value-emphases of Greek culture as:

holding the existential postulates that the
  universe is determinate and unitary and
  with evil more prominent than good;
believing that the individual has a measure
  of freedom and is morally accountable;
valuing the human as opposed to the supernatural;
  the individual as opposed to the group;
  the self versus the other;
  the present as opposed to either past or
  future;
valuing in different contexts both discipline
  and fulfillment.

This is, to be sure, only a very partial "grammar." I should have discussed at least three or four other value-pairs: intense versus bland, general versus particulars (Herodotus)—a "vibrant" culture as Mr. Robinson says, "it was the west [i.e. the Greeks] that placed emphasis on intangibles." I agree with Mr. Robinson that the spirit of the Athenians is still perhaps impossible to define, but trial must be made (Bowra). And I should have shown how the core values are congruent with what most of us would regard as the darker side of Greek culture—the position of women, slavery, fierce cruelty to other human beings on occasion. Nevertheless I do believe that the structural principles which I have considered do constitute in their thematic combinations an important portion of the "distinctive features" of Greek culture.

Now, finally, let me say—without straining for any kind of rigor—a few sentences which express what one anthropologist regards as the peculiar, overall character of Greek culture when compared with many others. The same thought can be expressed in several ways which all come down to the same thing. One can get at it through representative words of the Greeks such as Euripides' characterization of the glory of Athens as where "the loves mated to wisdom work all virtues."

Most briefly, it is the heroic idea of man. Partly outlined and adumbrated in Homer and fully present from the sixth century on, the distinctive Greek conception of human life was that of proud ("my hope treads not for me the halls of fear"; "there is the sea—who shall dry it up?") humanism. Looking intelligently but squarely at the totality of experience, seeking for *arete* which Aristotle called "the possession of the beautiful," Greek humanism at its finest—in Sophocles, for example—had a high-hearted and triumphant serenity which no God could sanctify nor devil violate.

Surely the legacy of Greece is, in Thucydides' phrase, a *ktema es aei,* "an imperishable possession," for all that shall live hereafter.

Modern References Cited

I

ADAMS, S. M.: *Sophocles the Playwright.* Toronto: University of Toronto Press. 1957. *The Phoenix,* Supplementary Vol. III.

BACHOFEN, J. J.: *Das Mutterrecht: Eine Untersuchung über die Gynaikokratie der alten Welt nach ihrer religiösen und rechtlichen Natur.* Stuttgart: Krais & Hoffmann. 1861.

BROWN, NORMAN: *Hermes the Thief: The Evolution of a Myth.* Madison: University of Wisconsin Press. 1947.

BURN, A. R.: *The World of Hesiod: A Study of the Greek Middle Ages, c. 900-700 B.C.* London: K. Paul, Trench, Trubner & Co., Ltd. 1936.

CARPENTER, RHYS: *Folk Tale, Fiction and Saga in the Homeric Epics.* Berkeley: University of California Press. 1946.

DODDS, E. R.: *The Greeks and the Irrational.* Berkeley: University of California Press. 1951.

FINLEY, M. I.: *The World of Odysseus.* New York: Viking Press. 1954.

FIRTH, RAYMOND W.: *Social Anthropology as Science and as Art.* Dunedin: University of Otago. 1958.

FORTES, MEYER: *Oedipus and Job in West African Religion.* Cambridge: University Press. 1959.

FRAZER, SIR JAMES GEORGE: *The Golden Bough.* 3rd ed., 1907-1915, in 12 volumes. London: Macmillan & Co.

———: *The New Golden Bough.* Ed. by Theodor H. Gaster. New York: Criterion Books. 1959.

FUSTEL DE COULANGES, NUMA DENIS: *La Cité Antique: Étude sur le culte, le droit, les institutions de la Grèce et de Rome.* Paris: L. Hachette et Cie. 1864.

69

HARRISON, JANE E.: *Themis: A Study of the Social Origins of Greek Religion.* Cambridge: University Press. 1912.

HENCKEN, H. O'NEILL: *Indo-European Languages and Archeology.* Menasha, Wisconsin: American Anthropological Association *Memoir* No. 84. 1955.

KROEBER, A. L.: *Configurations of Culture Growth.* Berkeley: University of California Press. 1944.

——: The Ancient Oikumene as a Historic Culture Aggregate. The Huxley Memorial Lecture for 1945. In *The Nature of Culture,* pp. 379-395. Chicago: University of Chicago Press. 1952.

——: Concluding Review in *An Appraisal of Anthropology Today,* Ed. by Sol Tax *et al.,* Chapter XX, pp. 357-376. Chicago: University of Chicago Press. 1953.

LANG, ANDREW: *The Making of Religion.* London: Longmans, Green, and Co. 1898.

LÉVI-STRAUSS, CLAUDE: The Structural Study of Myths. *Journal of American Folklore.* Vol. 68, No. 270, pp. 428-444. 1955.

LITTLE, ALAN M. G.: *Myth and Society in Attic Drama.* New York: Columbia University Press. 1942.

MAINE, SIR HENRY S.: *Ancient Law.* London: John Murray. 1861.

MARETT, R. R.: *Anthropology and the Classics.* Oxford: Clarendon Press. 1908.

McLENNAN, JOHN F.: *Studies in Ancient History.* New York: Macmillan and Co. 1886.

MORGAN, L. H.: *Ancient Society.* New York: Henry Holt & Company. 1877.

——: *Systems of Consanguinity and Affinity of the Human Family.* Washington, D.C.: Smithsonian Institution. 1870. *Smithsonian Contributions to Knowledge,* Vol. 17, art. 2.

MURRAY, GILBERT: *Five Stages of Greek Religion: Studies Based on a Course of Lectures Delivered in April 1912 at Columbia University.* Oxford: Clarendon Press. 1925.

MYRES, SIR JOHN L.: *Who Were the Greeks?* Berkeley: University of California Press. 1930.

ONIANS, R. B.: *The Origins of European Thought About the Body, the Mind, the Soul, the World, Time, and Fate: New Interpretations of Greek, Roman and Kindred Evidence, also of Some Basic Jewish and Christian Beliefs.* Cambridge: University Press. 1951.

——: Second edition. 1954.

PALMER, L. R.: *Achaeans and Indo-Europeans; An Inaugural Lecture, Delivered before the University of Oxford on 4 November 1954.* Oxford: Clarendon Press. 1955.

RIDGEWAY, SIR WILLIAM: *The Origin of Tragedy with Special Reference to the Greek Tragedians.* Cambridge: University Press. 1910.

ROHDE, ERWIN: *Psyche: Seelencult und Unsterblichkeitsglaube der Griechen.* Tübingen & Leipzig: J. C. B. Mohr. 1903.

———: *Psyche: the Cult of Souls and Belief in Immortality among the Greeks.* London: K. Paul, Trench, Trubner & Co., Ltd. 1925.

ROSE, H. J.: *Concerning Parallels.* The Frazer Lecture, 1934. Oxford: Clarendon Press. 1934.

SHOREY, PAUL: Review: *The Classical Tradition in Poetry, The Charles Eliot Norton Lectures.* By Gilbert Murray. Cambridge: Harvard University Press. Mimeographed copy. n.d.

SIKES, E. E.: *The Anthropology of the Greeks.* London: David Nutt. 1914.

TAX, SOL, et al.: *An Appraisal of Anthropology Today.* Chicago: University of Chicago Press. 1953.

THOMSON, GEORGE D.: *Aeschylus and Athens: A study in the Social Origins of Drama.* London: Lawrence & Wishart, Ltd. 1941.

———: *Studies in Ancient Greek Society.* Volume I. London: Lawrence & Wishart. 1949.

TYLOR, E .B.: *Anthropological Essays Presented to Edward Burnett Tylor in Honor of his 75th Birthday, Oct. 2, 1907,* by H. Balfour et al. Northcote W. Thomas, ed. Oxford: Clarendon Press. 1907.

USENER, HERMANN K.: Mythologie. *Archiv für Religionswissenschaft,* Band 7, pp. 6-32. Leipzig: B. G. Teubner. 1904.

II

BOAS, GEORGE: Some Assumptions of Aristotle. American Philosophical Society *Transactions.* New Series, Vol. 40, Part 6. Philadelphia: The American Philosophical Society. 1959.

DODDS, E. R.: *The Greeks and the Irrational.* Berkeley: University of California Press. 1951.

GREENE, WILLIAM CHASE: Platonism and Its Critics. *Harvard Studies in Classical Philology,* Vol. LXI, pp. 39-71. Cambridge. 1953.

JAEGER, WERNER W.: *Paideia: The Ideals of Greek Culture.* Volume I. Translated by Gilbert Highet. New York: Oxford University Press. 1939.

MYRES, SIR JOHN L.: The Sigynnae of Herodotus: An Ethnological Problem of the Early Iron Age. *Anthropological Essays Presented to Edward Burnett Tylor, Oct. 2, 1907.* Northcote W. Thomas, ed. Oxford: Clarendon Press. 1907.

ROBINSON, CHARLES A., JR.: *Athens in the Age of Pericles.* Norman: University of Oklahoma Press. 1959.

III

BECKER, CARL L.: *The Heavenly City of the Eighteenth Century Philosophers.* New Haven: Yale University Press. 1935.

BOWRA, C. M.: Review: *Humanism: The Greek Ideal and Its Survival,* by Moses Hadas. *New York Times Book Review,* March 20, p. 16. 1960.

FRIEDMANN, F. G., ed.: *The Peasant:* A Symposium Concerning the Peasant Way and View of Life. Number 7. Mimeographed. Fayetteville: Department of Philosophy, University of Arkansas. 1956.

GREENE, WILLIAM CHASE: *Moira: Fate, Good and Evil, in Greek Thought.* Cambridge: Harvard University Press. 1944.

HADAS, MOSES: *Humanism: The Greek Ideal and Its Survival.* New York: Harper & Bros. 1960.

PHILLIPS, HENRY, JR.: *De vocis hamartia vi et usu apud scriptores Graecos usque ad annum CCC ante Christum natum.* Harvard University, Graduate School of Arts and Sciences: *Summaries of Theses . . . for the Degree of Doctor of Philosophy,* 1933, pp. 9-11. Cambridge. 1934.

WHITMAN, CEDRIC H.: *Sophocles: A Study of Heroic Humanism.* Cambridge: Harvard University Press. 1951.

YOUNG, J. Z.: *Doubt and Certainty in Science: A Biologist's Reflections on the Brain.* Oxford: Clarendon Press. 1951.

Index

COMPOSED, PRINTED AND BOUND BY
GEORGE BANTA COMPANY, INC., MENASHA, WISCONSIN

This volume is printed on a stable and
enduring text paper developed under a
grant to the Virginia State Library by
the Council on Library Resources, Inc.